Comprehensive Guide to Cross-Platform Architecture

*Building Reliable, Scalable, and Agile Applications with Python and C#**

THOMPSON CARTER

Table of Content

TABLE OF CONTENTS

4

Introduction

In today's fast-paced world, software development is evolving rapidly, with cross-platform solutions becoming more and more essential. Developers, businesses, and organizations are constantly looking for efficient ways to build applications that work seamlessly across multiple platforms—whether mobile, web, or desktop—without compromising on performance or user experience. Cross-platform development is no longer a niche skill but a fundamental approach to building modern software applications.

This book, **"Comprehensive Guide to Cross-Platform Architecture: Building Reliable, Scalable, and Agile Applications with Python and C#"**, is designed to give you a comprehensive understanding of cross-platform development, focusing on the strengths of two of the most popular programming languages today—**Python** and **C#**. Whether you're a beginner just entering the world of cross-platform development, or an experienced developer looking to expand your skillset, this book is structured to guide you through the core concepts, best practices, and tools you need to master cross-platform application development.

6

Why Cross-Platform Development?

The demand for applications that can work across multiple platforms (Android, iOS, Windows, macOS, Web) has skyrocketed. Developing separate applications for each platform can be costly and time-consuming. Cross-platform development solves this problem by allowing developers to write a single codebase that can be deployed on various platforms, saving both time and resources. However, this approach comes with its own set of challenges, from performance issues to platform-specific inconsistencies.

This book addresses these challenges head-on, offering solutions and insights into how to design, build, and deploy applications that are reliable, scalable, and agile across multiple environments. We cover everything from the fundamental principles of cross-platform architecture to advanced techniques for creating high-performance, enterprise-grade applications.

What Will You Learn from This Book?

By reading this book, you will gain a deep understanding of cross-platform architecture and development using **Python** and **C#**, two of the most widely used programming languages in the industry today. Throughout the chapters, we will walk you through the following key topics:

1. **Cross-Platform Fundamentals**: You will start by understanding the foundational concepts of cross-platform development, including the various platforms, environments, and frameworks available to developers. You'll learn about the differences between mobile, desktop, and web platforms and how to manage them effectively within a single codebase.

2. **Building Reliable, Scalable, and Agile Applications**: Learn how to design applications that can handle growing user bases and traffic while maintaining high performance. You will explore techniques for scaling applications horizontally and vertically, implementing redundancy and fault tolerance, and ensuring high availability.

3. **Agile Methodologies**: Cross-platform development requires an efficient development process, and Agile methodologies play a significant role in managing such projects. You will learn how to integrate Agile principles into cross-platform development workflows, ensuring faster and more flexible delivery of features.

4. **Performance Optimization**: Performance is crucial in cross-platform development. We will delve into performance profiling, handling bottlenecks, and using the right tools and techniques to ensure your applications run smoothly across all platforms.

5. **UI/UX Design**: Designing intuitive, responsive, and native-like user interfaces across multiple platforms can be challenging. This book covers best practices for creating consistent and engaging UI/UX designs that cater to the unique requirements of each platform while maintaining a cohesive experience.

6. **Real-World Case Studies**: To provide a practical context, we analyze successful real-world cross-platform projects and dissect the tools, technologies, and methodologies used by companies to build reliable and high-performing applications.

7. **Debugging and Troubleshooting**: Debugging in a cross-platform environment can be tricky. We cover the best practices and tools for identifying and solving common issues that arise in cross-platform development, ensuring your app works perfectly across all platforms.

8. **Emerging Technologies**: As cross-platform development continues to evolve, emerging

technologies like AI, machine learning, and augmented reality are playing an increasing role. This book will provide insights into how you can incorporate these technologies into your cross-platform apps.

9. **Mastering Python and C# for Cross-Platform Development**: Throughout the book, you will explore the advantages of Python and C# in the context of cross-platform development. You will learn how both languages are evolving to support modern app architectures, how to leverage their respective frameworks and tools, and how to write clean, maintainable code that can run on multiple platforms.

Who Is This Book For?

This book is aimed at anyone who wants to understand the intricacies of cross-platform development, whether you are a:

- **Beginner Developer**: If you're new to development or cross-platform frameworks, this book will give you a solid foundation in how to create applications that work seamlessly across mobile, desktop, and web platforms.

- **Experienced Developer**: If you already have experience in building single-platform applications and are looking to transition into cross-platform development, this book will provide you with the advanced tools and knowledge to take your skills to the next level.
- **Software Architect**: For software architects who need to design and implement scalable, reliable, and efficient cross-platform systems, this book will provide strategies for building cross-platform solutions that work across a wide range of devices and platforms.

Why Focus on Python and C#?

Python is a versatile and easy-to-learn language, which makes it an excellent choice for rapid prototyping, web development, and data-intensive applications. Although Python has traditionally been seen as a back-end or scripting language, its rich ecosystem of libraries and frameworks has allowed it to expand into mobile and desktop app development. Frameworks like **Kivy**, **BeeWare**, and **PyQt** allow Python developers to build fully-functional cross-platform apps.

C#, on the other hand, is a mature and powerful language primarily known for its role in enterprise applications and game development (via **Unity**). **Xamarin** allows C#

developers to write mobile applications for both **iOS** and **Android** using a single codebase. Combined with its strong integration with the **.NET** ecosystem and cloud services like **Azure**, C# is one of the best languages for developing large-scale, cross-platform applications.

By focusing on both **Python** and **C#**, this book equips you with the skills and knowledge to use the right language and framework for your project, regardless of its scale or complexity.

Structure of the Book

This book is divided into 20 chapters, each focusing on a specific aspect of cross-platform development:

1. **Introduction to Cross-Platform Development**
2. **Understanding Cross-Platform Architecture**
3. **The Role of Python and C# in Cross-Platform Development**
4. **Building Scalable Applications**
5. **Designing Reliable Systems**
6. **Agile Methodologies for Cross-Platform Development**
7. **Performance Optimization Across Platforms**
8. **Effective Testing Strategies**
9. **Cross-Platform Tools and Frameworks**

10. **Cloud Integration in Cross-Platform Development**
11. **Managing Data in Cross-Platform Applications**
12. **Security in Cross-Platform Systems**
13. **Continuous Integration and Continuous Deployment (CI/CD)**
14. **Managing API Integrations**
15. **UI/UX Design in Cross-Platform Applications**
16. **Troubleshooting Cross-Platform Issues**
17. **Future Trends in Cross-Platform Architecture**
18. **Building Cross-Platform Mobile Applications**
19. **Case Studies of Successful Cross-Platform Projects**
20. **Conclusion and Next Steps**

Each chapter will provide practical knowledge, real-world examples, and actionable insights that you can apply directly to your own cross-platform projects. Whether you are building a small app or designing a large-scale enterprise solution, this book provides the tools, techniques, and strategies you need to succeed.

Conclusion

By the end of this book, you will have a deep understanding of cross-platform development and be equipped with the skills to build applications that work across multiple platforms efficiently. You'll have the tools and knowledge to tackle the challenges that arise in cross-platform development, as well as the foresight to incorporate emerging technologies into your applications.

As you embark on your journey into cross-platform development, remember that continuous learning, experimentation, and hands-on practice are key. This book is your starting point, but the real growth comes from applying what you've learned in real-world projects. Happy coding!

CHAPTER 1

INTRODUCTION TO CROSS-PLATFORM DEVELOPMENT

Overview of Cross-Platform Development

Cross-platform development refers to the practice of creating applications that can run on multiple operating systems and devices without needing to be rewritten for each one. The aim is to build a single codebase that works seamlessly across various platforms, such as Windows, macOS, Linux, Android, and iOS. This approach simplifies development, reduces costs, and accelerates time to market.

In cross-platform development, the focus is on reusing the same codebase across different platforms, ensuring that the application's functionality, design, and user experience remain consistent. With the evolution of modern software tools and frameworks, developers can now create applications that are portable and adaptive, without sacrificing performance or user experience.

Why It's Essential for Modern Applications

Cross-platform development has become increasingly crucial due to the growing diversity in user devices and operating systems. With so many platforms available, companies cannot afford to develop separate applications for each system.

Some key reasons why cross-platform development is essential for modern applications include:

- **Cost-Effectiveness**: Writing separate applications for each platform can be expensive. Cross-platform development allows teams to focus on one codebase, which can be deployed across multiple platforms, significantly reducing costs.
- **Faster Time-to-Market**: By developing a single application for all platforms, developers can roll out new features or updates faster. The unified codebase streamlines testing, debugging, and deployment processes.
- **Wider Audience Reach**: By supporting multiple platforms, applications can reach a larger audience, expanding their user base and improving engagement.
- **Consistency**: Cross-platform development ensures that users across different platforms have similar experiences.

It helps maintain consistency in performance, user interface, and design, which is crucial for building a strong brand identity.

Key Concepts: Platforms, Environments, and Frameworks

To successfully implement cross-platform development, it's essential to understand the key concepts of platforms, environments, and frameworks:

- **Platforms**: These are the operating systems or hardware environments where applications run. Common platforms include Windows, macOS, Linux, Android, and iOS. Each platform has unique requirements and limitations, making it challenging to develop applications that work seamlessly on all.

- **Environments**: This refers to the software tools, libraries, and APIs that allow applications to interact with the underlying platform. Development environments, such as Integrated Development Environments (IDEs) and toolchains, play a critical role in simplifying the development and debugging process.

- **Frameworks**: Frameworks are pre-built structures that provide essential building blocks for applications. These tools offer a set of libraries and functions, speeding up the development process and making it easier to handle cross-platform issues. Some examples include:

- o **.NET Core** for C# developers, which enables building cross-platform applications.
- o **Flutter**, **React Native**, or **Xamarin** for mobile app development.
- o **Django** or **Flask** for Python developers focusing on web applications.

Introduction to Python and C# in Cross-Platform Architecture

Python and C# are two powerful programming languages that have gained prominence in the realm of cross-platform development due to their versatility, ease of use, and rich ecosystems of libraries and frameworks.

- **Python**: Python is widely known for its simplicity and readability, making it an ideal choice for developers who want to quickly develop applications that can run across multiple platforms. Libraries such as **Kivy** and **BeeWare** are designed specifically for building cross-platform applications. Python is a great choice for developing web applications,

18

command-line tools, desktop applications, and even mobile apps with the right frameworks.

- **C#**: C# is a robust, object-oriented programming language developed by Microsoft. It has been a core component of the .NET framework, which provides powerful tools for cross-platform development. With the advent of **.NET Core**, C# has become an excellent choice for developing cross-platform applications. Frameworks like **Xamarin** allow developers to create mobile apps that work across Android and iOS with a single C# codebase. Additionally, C# is used for creating server-side applications, desktop software, and even games using Unity.

Both Python and C# offer extensive libraries and frameworks that make cross-platform development more accessible, reducing the complexity of working with multiple platforms.

Key Takeaways

- Cross-platform development enables the creation of applications that run on multiple platforms using a single codebase, saving time, money, and effort.

- Modern applications need to be cross-platform to meet the demands of diverse user bases, improve user experiences, and stay competitive.

- Key concepts like platforms, environments, and frameworks shape how cross-platform development is approached, with tools like **.NET Core**, **Kivy**, and **Xamarin** streamlining the process.

- Python and C# are leading languages in cross-platform development, offering developers the flexibility to create scalable, reliable, and feature-rich applications across multiple platforms.

By the end of this chapter, you should have a clear understanding of the importance and benefits of cross-platform development and how Python and C# play a critical role in making this possible.

CHAPTER 2

UNDERSTANDING CROSS-PLATFORM ARCHITECTURE

What Cross-Platform Architecture Entails

Cross-platform architecture refers to the design and structure of software applications that are intended to run on multiple platforms, such as Windows, macOS, Linux, Android, and iOS, without the need for platform-specific code for each. It involves using frameworks, tools, and strategies that ensure the application behaves consistently and efficiently across all platforms, while maintaining a single codebase.

At the core of cross-platform architecture is the idea of portability and adaptability, which allows developers to build applications that can seamlessly transition between different environments. The architecture must account for various aspects such as operating systems, hardware, user interfaces, performance, and data synchronization, ensuring that each platform can handle the app effectively.

The key challenge in cross-platform architecture is ensuring that the user experience (UX) and functionality are not compromised, even though the same code is used across different platforms. This requires careful design of the software's backend, frontend, and overall system, leveraging cross-platform tools and frameworks.

Key Architectural Patterns: Microservices, Monolithic, and Serverless

When designing cross-platform applications, different architectural patterns can be used depending on the application's size, complexity, and requirements. These include **microservices**, **monolithic**, and **serverless** architectures. Let's break each one down:

1. **Microservices Architecture**
   - **Overview**: Microservices architecture divides an application into small, independent services that communicate over a network. Each service performs a specific function and can be deployed and updated independently of the others.
   - **How it fits with cross-platform**: Microservices allow different parts of an application to be built and deployed across various platforms, ensuring that each service can operate in the most appropriate environment. Each service could be developed using a different technology stack,

22

such as Python or C#, and run in separate containers or environments.

- o **Benefits**:
  - Scalability: Each service can be scaled independently.
  - Flexibility: Developers can choose the best technology stack for each service.
  - Fault isolation: A failure in one service does not affect the entire application.
- o **Challenges**:
  - Complexity: Managing multiple services, databases, and dependencies can be complex.
  - Communication overhead: Microservices need robust communication mechanisms (such as APIs) to work together.

2. **Monolithic Architecture**
   - o **Overview**: A monolithic architecture refers to a unified model where all components of an application are integrated into a single codebase and deployed together. In a monolithic system, different parts of the application (frontend, backend, database, etc.) share the same infrastructure.

- o **How it fits with cross-platform**: For smaller or less complex applications, a monolithic architecture might be more suitable for cross-platform development. A single application can be built and run across multiple platforms using tools like Xamarin, Flutter, or Django.
- o **Benefits**:
  - Simplicity: The application is built and deployed as a single unit, making development easier for small teams.
  - Easier debugging: Since everything is integrated, tracing issues within the code is simpler.
- o **Challenges**:
  - Scalability: As the application grows, scaling becomes difficult and expensive.
  - Limited flexibility: Changes to one part of the system might require redeployment of the entire application, which can slow down development.

3. **Serverless Architecture**
   - o **Overview**: Serverless architecture allows developers to build and run applications without managing the underlying infrastructure. Instead, cloud providers offer functions that run in

response to events and automatically scale based on demand.

- o **How it fits with cross-platform**: Serverless can be ideal for cross-platform development as it abstracts the platform layer, enabling the code to run across different cloud environments. Serverless applications can easily scale and adjust resources based on platform needs.
- o **Benefits**:
  - Cost-effective: You only pay for the execution time of functions, rather than provisioning servers.
  - Automatic scaling: The application automatically scales based on usage, making it ideal for fluctuating workloads.
- o **Challenges**:
  - Vendor lock-in: Using a specific cloud provider's serverless platform might make it difficult to migrate to another provider.
  - Cold starts: Serverless functions might have latency issues due to "cold starts," where functions take longer to respond if not called frequently.

Benefits and Challenges of Cross-Platform Design

Developing cross-platform applications offers many advantages, but it also comes with its own set of challenges. Let's examine both:

Benefits

1. **Cost Efficiency**: The biggest advantage of cross-platform development is the ability to write a single codebase and deploy it across multiple platforms. This eliminates the need for separate teams to write different code for each operating system, significantly reducing development and maintenance costs.

2. **Faster Development and Deployment**: With a single codebase, updates and bug fixes can be implemented across all platforms simultaneously, which leads to faster time-to-market. It also allows developers to maintain a consistent user experience and feature set on all platforms.

3. **Wider Reach**: Cross-platform applications can be deployed across multiple platforms, ensuring that the application is accessible to a larger audience. This is particularly important for businesses that want to

target both desktop and mobile users, or even different operating systems, like Windows, macOS, Linux, Android, and iOS.

4. **Consistency in User Experience**: One of the most critical aspects of cross-platform development is providing a consistent user experience across all platforms. With cross-platform tools, developers can ensure that the interface, layout, and functionality are uniform, no matter where the application runs.

5. **Easier Maintenance**: Maintaining a single codebase instead of multiple codebases reduces the complexity and overhead associated with updates, bug fixes, and improvements. It also makes it easier to test and ensure that any changes are applied uniformly across all platforms.

Challenges

1. **Performance Limitations**: Cross-platform applications sometimes suffer from performance issues due to the abstraction layer required for portability. Native applications can optimize resource use and performance, while cross-platform apps may experience delays or lag, especially when

dealing with heavy computational tasks or complex graphics.

2. **Platform-Specific Issues**: Even with cross-platform frameworks, some platform-specific issues can arise. These may include UI inconsistencies, performance issues, or platform-specific features that are difficult to implement consistently across all platforms.

3. **Lack of Access to Native Features**: Cross-platform development frameworks often provide limited access to native device capabilities, such as sensors, camera functionalities, or specific platform APIs. If your application requires deep integration with the operating system or hardware, cross-platform frameworks may not fully meet your needs.

4. **Debugging and Testing Complexity**: Debugging cross-platform applications can be challenging because bugs might manifest differently across platforms. Testing becomes more complex as well, requiring testing on multiple platforms to ensure consistency.

5. **Dependency on Frameworks and Tools**: While cross-platform frameworks provide useful tools, they can also lock developers into specific tools or libraries. This can become problematic if the

toolchain or framework is no longer maintained or does not support a new version of a platform.

Key Takeaways

- Cross-platform architecture enables developers to create applications that can run on multiple platforms using a single codebase, ensuring consistency and reducing development costs.
- Different architectural patterns, such as **microservices**, **monolithic**, and **serverless**, each have their pros and cons when applied to cross-platform development.
- The benefits of cross-platform design include cost savings, faster development, a wider audience reach, and easier maintenance, while the challenges mainly involve performance limitations, platform-specific issues, and the complexity of debugging.

By understanding these architectural patterns and the advantages and challenges of cross-platform design, you can make informed decisions when architecting your next cross-platform application.

CHAPTER 3

THE ROLE OF PYTHON AND C# IN CROSS-PLATFORM DEVELOPMENT

Strengths of Python and C# in Cross-Platform Projects

Both Python and C# have established themselves as popular programming languages for cross-platform development. While each has unique strengths, their capabilities make them suitable for building scalable, reliable, and high-performance applications across various platforms.

Strengths of Python

1. **Simplicity and Readability**: Python is known for its clean and readable syntax, which makes it one of the most beginner-friendly languages. Its simple structure allows developers to quickly pick it up and start building applications, saving both time and resources. This is especially important in cross-platform development, where clarity in code leads to fewer errors and smoother collaboration.

2. **Rich Ecosystem and Libraries**: Python offers an extensive collection of libraries and frameworks, which simplifies the development of cross-platform applications. Libraries such as **Kivy**, **BeeWare**, and **PyQt** are specifically designed for building native-like applications across multiple platforms (including Windows, macOS, Linux, and mobile operating systems). Python also integrates well with various cloud platforms, making it suitable for cloud-based cross-platform applications.

3. **Versatility**: Python is incredibly versatile, supporting various application types, including web development (using **Flask** or **Django**), machine learning (with libraries like **TensorFlow** and **scikit-learn**), and automation tasks. This makes it a go-to language for cross-platform projects that span across different domains and technologies.

4. **Cross-Platform Tools**: With frameworks like **PyInstaller** and **cx_Freeze**, Python can easily be packaged into standalone executables that work across different operating systems. Additionally, tools like **PyQt** allow developers to create applications with graphical user interfaces (GUIs) that are portable across different environments.

Strengths of C#

1. **Strong Support for Microsoft Platforms**: As a language developed by Microsoft, C# is naturally strong in environments like **Windows, Azure**, and **.NET**. However, with the introduction of **.NET Core**, C# has become a robust cross-platform solution, enabling developers to build applications for **Windows, Linux**, and **macOS** without rewriting code for each platform.

2. **Integrated Development Environment (IDE)**: One of the biggest advantages of using C# is the development environment. **Visual Studio** is an industry-leading IDE that provides comprehensive debugging tools, a rich library of templates, and a powerful editor that significantly boosts developer productivity, especially in cross-platform projects. Visual Studio's ability to target multiple platforms directly from the IDE makes C# an excellent choice for developers working in cross-platform scenarios.

3. **Strong Typing and Performance**: C# is a statically typed language, which results in fewer runtime errors and better code optimization. When performance is critical, such as in game development or high-performance computing applications, C# can deliver

faster execution times compared to dynamically typed languages like Python.

4. **Cross-Platform Mobile Development with Xamarin**: With **Xamarin**, C# can be used to build native mobile applications for **Android** and **iOS** using a single codebase. Xamarin provides access to native device features, offering a seamless mobile experience while reducing development time and cost. This makes C# a top choice for developers looking to target both mobile and desktop platforms simultaneously.

5. **Large Ecosystem and Community Support**: Like Python, C# has a large and active community of developers and a wide range of third-party libraries and frameworks. The **.NET Core** ecosystem has grown substantially, and tools like **Xamarin**, **ASP.NET Core**, and **Blazor** allow developers to build scalable web, desktop, and mobile applications.

Choosing the Right Language for the Job

When deciding whether to use Python or C# for a cross-platform project, it's important to consider the nature of the project, the skillset of the development team, and the target platforms. Here are some factors to consider when choosing the right language:

1. **Project Type**:
   - o If you are building a **web application** or need to work with **data science**, **machine learning**, or **automation**, Python is a strong choice. Its vast array of frameworks (like Django or Flask for web development) and its role in the scientific computing space make it ideal for data-driven, web-based, and automation tasks.
   - o For **enterprise-level applications**, **mobile applications**, or **games**, C# might be the better choice. Its performance optimizations and the ability to target multiple platforms with **Xamarin** or **Unity** for game development make C# a go-to language for these use cases.

2. **Team Expertise**:
   - o Python is often preferred by teams with experience in data-driven fields, such as research, artificial intelligence, or automation, due to its simpler syntax and extensive libraries.
   - o If the development team is already familiar with Microsoft technologies or is focused on performance-critical applications, C# would be a

natural fit due to its integration with the **.NET** ecosystem and its powerful development tools.

3. **Target Platforms**:

   o Python is great for building **cross-platform desktop** applications and server-side applications, especially for Linux, macOS, and Windows. If your application does not require deep native mobile support or high-performance capabilities, Python can be a great choice.

   o C# shines when developing **mobile applications** (through **Xamarin**) or **enterprise applications** that require integration with Microsoft's services or rely heavily on Windows-based environments. Additionally, if your application needs high performance or is expected to scale to millions of users, C# provides better tools for optimization.

4. **Performance Needs**:

   o If the application is performance-critical (such as games, real-time processing, or high-frequency trading systems), C# may be a better choice due to its faster execution time and better memory management in comparison to Python.

   o For applications where performance is not a primary concern, Python's simplicity and speed of development might be preferred.

Real-World Examples Where Each Excels

1. **Python**:
    - o **Dropbox**: Dropbox, the popular cloud storage service, uses Python for its server-side architecture, primarily for its simplicity and efficiency. The ability to write cross-platform code using Python helped Dropbox scale quickly while maintaining code consistency across platforms.
    - o **Instagram**: Instagram's backend is powered by Python, using Django as the web framework. The choice of Python was driven by the need for rapid development and easy maintenance, allowing Instagram to scale as the user base grew.
    - o **Spotify**: Spotify also leverages Python for backend services, particularly for data processing and machine learning algorithms, thanks to Python's rich ecosystem in data science and analytics.

2. **C#**:
    - o **Microsoft Teams**: C# is used extensively in Microsoft Teams to provide a seamless, cross-platform experience for users. By using **.NET Core**, Microsoft was able to extend Teams across

various platforms, including Windows, macOS, and mobile devices.

- **Xamarin Apps**: Applications built using **Xamarin** (such as **Alaska Airlines** mobile app or **The World Bank's app**) show how C# can be used to create native mobile apps for both Android and iOS. These apps are efficient and easy to maintain due to Xamarin's unified codebase.

- **Unity Games**: C# is the primary language used in **Unity**, one of the most widely used game engines. Games like **Angry Birds 2** and **Pokémon Go** were developed using C# and Unity, highlighting the language's effectiveness in creating performance-optimized mobile and desktop games.

Key Takeaways

- **Python** is ideal for rapid development, data-driven applications, and web services, with frameworks like Django and Flask offering easy portability across different platforms.

- **C#** is a powerful choice for building performance-sensitive applications, including mobile apps with Xamarin, desktop software, and games with Unity, making it a great option for large-scale, enterprise-level cross-platform development.

- Choosing the right language depends on the project type, the expertise of the development team, and the specific platform requirements.

Both Python and C# offer compelling features for cross-platform development. Understanding the strengths and limitations of each allows developers to make informed decisions that best suit the needs of their project.

CHAPTER 4

BUILDING SCALABLE APPLICATIONS

Concepts of Scalability in Cross-Platform Development

Scalability is a critical concept in cross-platform development, particularly when applications need to handle increasing workloads, large numbers of users, or fluctuating demands. In simple terms, scalability refers to the ability of a system to handle growing amounts of work or to be easily expanded to accommodate growth. For cross-platform applications, scalability ensures that the application can maintain performance, availability, and responsiveness across multiple platforms, whether it's a desktop, mobile, or cloud-based app.

There are two main aspects of scalability:

1. **Performance Scalability**: This refers to the system's ability to maintain or improve its performance as the load increases, such as handling more users, more data, or more transactions per second.

2. **Capacity Scalability**: This focuses on the system's ability to grow in terms of resources like storage, compute power, or network capacity without affecting the application's performance.

For cross-platform applications, scalability isn't just about handling more users on one platform, but ensuring the app can perform well across various platforms—Windows, macOS, Android, iOS, or web—without the need for substantial platform-specific changes.

Key challenges in building scalable cross-platform applications include maintaining uniform performance across platforms, efficiently managing resources, and ensuring the system remains responsive under different load conditions.

Horizontal vs Vertical Scaling

When scaling applications, two primary approaches are used: **horizontal scaling** and **vertical scaling**. Each approach has its own advantages and trade-offs, and the choice between them depends on the architecture of the application and the resources available.

40

Horizontal Scaling

Horizontal scaling, also known as **scaling out**, involves adding more machines or nodes to a system. Instead of upgrading a single machine, you add multiple machines or instances that work together to handle the increased load. In cloud computing, this can mean adding more virtual machines, containers, or microservices.

- **How it works**: The application is distributed across multiple servers, which share the load. The load balancer distributes traffic evenly across the available servers to ensure no single server is overwhelmed.
- **Benefits**:
  - **Resilience**: Horizontal scaling increases fault tolerance. If one node fails, the others continue to function, ensuring high availability.
  - **Elasticity**: Cloud environments make horizontal scaling easy, allowing resources to be scaled up or down automatically based on demand.
  - **Better handling of large-scale workloads**: This approach is suitable for applications that need to handle a large number of concurrent users or requests.
- **Challenges**:

o **Complexity**: Managing multiple nodes and ensuring they communicate effectively can be complex. This may require robust infrastructure tools and monitoring systems.

o **Data consistency**: Distributing data across multiple nodes requires ensuring data consistency and synchronization, which can introduce overhead.

Vertical Scaling

Vertical scaling, also known as **scaling up**, involves adding more resources (CPU, memory, or storage) to an existing server to improve its performance. This is a simpler form of scaling, where a single machine or node is upgraded to handle increased loads.

- **How it works**: The system's existing hardware is upgraded, such as adding more RAM or processing power, to improve its capacity to handle more load.
- **Benefits**:
  o **Simplicity**: Vertical scaling is generally simpler to implement because it doesn't require changes to the architecture. The application continues to run on a single server.

- o **Lower latency**: Since everything is on one machine, communication between components can be faster, reducing latency.
- **Challenges**:
  - o **Limited growth**: There's a physical limit to how much a single server can be upgraded. Once the machine reaches its limits, vertical scaling becomes inefficient or impossible.
  - o **Single point of failure**: If the single server fails, the entire application may go down, which could result in downtime and lost availability.

Which to Choose?

- **Horizontal scaling** is typically the better choice for cross-platform applications that need to handle large amounts of concurrent users or services. It's well-suited for cloud environments where the infrastructure can grow or shrink based on demand.
- **Vertical scaling** may be more appropriate for smaller applications or those that don't require the complexity of distributed systems. It's typically used for applications that are hosted on a single server or those that are in the early stages of growth.

43

Using Python and C# to Build Scalable Applications

Both Python and C# offer tools and frameworks that make it easier to build scalable applications, though they each have their strengths and are suited to different use cases.

Using Python for Scalability

1. **Web Frameworks**: Python has several web frameworks that help scale applications effectively. **Django** and **Flask** are two popular frameworks that can be used to build web applications capable of handling large traffic volumes.

   o **Django**: Django is a high-level Python framework that includes built-in components for building scalable, secure applications. Its **scalability features** include support for database sharding, caching, and integration with cloud services.

   o **Flask**: While Flask is lightweight and minimal, it allows for great flexibility in how you scale your application. Flask integrates well with other tools like **Celery** for background tasks and **Nginx** for load balancing.

2. **Asynchronous Programming**: Python's **asyncio** library allows developers to build scalable

44

applications that can handle thousands of simultaneous I/O-bound operations without blocking. Frameworks like **FastAPI** use async programming to support high-performance, scalable API services.

3. **Containerization and Orchestration**: Tools like **Docker** and **Kubernetes** are essential for deploying scalable Python applications. Docker allows you to package Python applications into containers, which can then be orchestrated and scaled with Kubernetes.

4. **Cloud Integration**: Python integrates well with cloud platforms like **AWS**, **Azure**, and **Google Cloud**. These platforms offer elastic scaling and managed services, allowing Python applications to automatically scale based on load.

Using C# for Scalability

1. **.NET Core**: C# with **.NET Core** provides a powerful and flexible platform for building scalable, cross-platform applications. .NET Core applications are inherently lightweight and fast, making them suitable for handling high-performance workloads.

   o **ASP.NET Core** is widely used for building scalable web applications, offering support for high-performance networking, multi-threading, and asynchronous programming.

2. **Xamarin for Mobile Apps**: **Xamarin** allows C# developers to write mobile applications that scale across both Android and iOS. Xamarin's **cross-platform capabilities** allow the same codebase to scale to multiple devices, and cloud services can be used to manage backend scaling.

3. **Microservices**: C# is well-suited for building microservices, which inherently scale horizontally. Using **Docker** and **Kubernetes** with .NET Core allows developers to break applications into smaller services, making scaling easier. Each microservice can be scaled independently based on demand.

4. **Cloud Integration with Azure**: C# developers working with **Azure** have the advantage of using a suite of cloud-based services that allow for seamless scaling. **Azure App Services** and **Azure Functions** can handle serverless computing and auto-scaling, which can improve the scalability of C# applications.

Real-World Examples of Scalable Applications

1. **Python**:

- o **Instagram**: Instagram's backend is built using Python and the **Django** framework, which scales effectively to handle millions of users worldwide. They use **horizontal scaling** with microservices to manage traffic, and **Redis** for caching, ensuring fast load times.

- o **Spotify**: Spotify uses Python to manage data processing and backend services. With tools like **Apache Kafka**, they scale their system horizontally, processing petabytes of music data and serving millions of users.

2. **C#**:

- o **Microsoft Azure**: The Azure cloud platform, primarily built using C#, provides scalable services such as **Azure App Services**, which can auto-scale based on demand. It handles millions of requests per second and ensures high availability through **horizontal scaling**.

- o **Stack Overflow**: The popular Q&A platform uses **C# and ASP.NET Core** for building scalable web applications. They scale horizontally by adding servers to meet the growing traffic demands while maintaining low latency and high availability.

Key Takeaways

- Scalability is crucial in cross-platform development to handle growing user bases and varying workloads. Understanding horizontal and vertical scaling helps in choosing the right strategy for your application.
- Python and C# both provide frameworks and tools to build scalable applications. Python excels in rapid development and handling asynchronous workloads, while C# offers high-performance solutions, particularly in cloud environments.
- Real-world examples like Instagram, Spotify, and Microsoft Azure demonstrate how Python and C# can be used to build scalable systems, each leveraging different architectural strategies to ensure seamless performance across platforms.

By leveraging the strengths of Python and C#, developers can build scalable applications that perform well across multiple platforms, ensuring a smooth experience for users no matter how much traffic the system handles.

CHAPTER 5

DESIGNING RELIABLE SYSTEMS

Reliability in Cross-Platform Systems

Reliability is one of the most critical attributes of any software system, particularly in cross-platform development. A reliable system performs consistently and accurately, providing users with a seamless experience across multiple platforms—whether it's a web, desktop, or mobile app. In cross-platform applications, reliability means ensuring that the app works flawlessly across all target platforms (e.g., Windows, macOS, Linux, Android, iOS), handling different environments and user behaviors without crashing, losing data, or causing errors.

Key challenges to reliability in cross-platform systems include:

- **Platform Inconsistencies**: Different platforms may have varying behaviors, system resources, and limitations, which can lead to unexpected errors if not properly managed.

- **Third-Party Dependencies**: Cross-platform applications often rely on third-party libraries or services, which may introduce bugs or break functionality when updated.
- **Complex Interactions**: Cross-platform systems may involve intricate interactions between different services, databases, APIs, and devices, which can increase the chances of failures.

To ensure reliability in these systems, developers must design applications with fault tolerance, error handling, and redundancy in mind. This requires anticipating potential points of failure and building mechanisms that allow the system to recover without affecting the user experience.

Fault Tolerance and Redundancy Strategies

Fault tolerance is the ability of a system to continue functioning properly even when one or more of its components fail. In cross-platform applications, where multiple environments and services are involved, implementing fault tolerance is crucial for maintaining reliability. Redundancy, on the other hand, involves duplicating critical components to ensure that the failure of one does not bring down the entire system.

Fault Tolerance Strategies

1. **Graceful Degradation**: Graceful degradation ensures that when a part of the system fails, the application continues to operate in a limited but functional state. For example, if a non-essential service or feature fails in a cross-platform app, the app should still allow users to perform core tasks while informing them of the issue.

2. **Retry Logic**: In the event of a failure (such as a temporary loss of network connectivity or an external API failure), the system can automatically retry the operation a set number of times before reporting an error. This ensures that transient issues do not affect the user experience.

3. **Circuit Breakers**: A circuit breaker pattern helps prevent a failure from cascading through the system. If a particular service or component fails multiple times in a row, the circuit breaker will "trip," temporarily halting further attempts to access that service and allowing the system to recover. Once the service is healthy again, the circuit breaker resets.

4. **Error Handling and Logging**: Proper error handling and logging mechanisms are essential for ensuring fault tolerance. When errors occur, the

system should catch them gracefully, log the details, and either continue or inform the user in a non-disruptive manner. This helps in identifying and fixing issues without compromising the overall functionality of the app.

Redundancy Strategies

1. **Replication**: Replicating data and services across multiple servers ensures that if one instance fails, another can take over without causing downtime. For instance, in a cloud-based system, you might replicate databases across multiple availability zones to prevent data loss and ensure high availability.

2. **Load Balancing**: Load balancing distributes traffic across multiple servers or instances to prevent any single server from becoming overwhelmed. This increases the reliability of the application by ensuring even traffic distribution and preventing performance degradation.

3. **Backup Systems**: Redundant backup systems store copies of essential data and configurations. For critical applications, regular backups ensure that, even in the case of data corruption or system failures,

the application can quickly recover with minimal data loss.

4. **Failover Systems**: A failover system automatically switches to a backup or secondary system when the primary system fails. This is particularly useful in cross-platform applications where uptime is critical. For example, cloud-based applications often use failover strategies to switch between different cloud regions or data centers if one becomes unavailable.

Tools and Techniques for Ensuring Reliability with Python and C#

Both Python and C# provide various tools and techniques to help developers design reliable systems. These tools focus on improving error handling, logging, fault tolerance, and overall application resilience.

Python Tools and Techniques

1. **Logging with Python**: Python's built-in **logging** module is a versatile tool for tracking events, exceptions, and errors in a system. By logging important events, developers can track system health, troubleshoot issues, and gain insights into how the system is performing across different platforms.

- o Use logging levels (e.g., DEBUG, INFO, WARNING, ERROR, CRITICAL) to capture varying degrees of events.
- o For cross-platform reliability, make sure logs are centralized for easy access, especially when dealing with distributed systems.

2. **Fault Tolerance with `retrying` and `tenacity`**: Python has third-party libraries like **retrying** and **tenacity**, which provide easy-to-implement retry logic for handling temporary failures. These libraries allow developers to specify retry policies (e.g., retry after N seconds or N times) and automatically handle errors when a service becomes temporarily unavailable.

3. **Celery for Distributed Task Management**: **Celery** is a distributed task queue that allows developers to execute tasks asynchronously, outside of the main application thread. It's commonly used for handling background tasks, such as sending emails or processing large datasets, without blocking the main application. Celery is highly scalable and fault-tolerant, ensuring tasks are retried or processed on a different worker if one fails.

4. **Docker and Kubernetes**: For building fault-tolerant, redundant systems, **Docker** and

Kubernetes are essential tools in Python-based applications. Docker containers encapsulate your application and its environment, while Kubernetes orchestrates the scaling, failover, and load balancing of containers, making it easier to design cross-platform systems that are highly available and fault-tolerant.

C# Tools and Techniques

1. **Logging with NLog or Serilog**: In C#, **NLog** and **Serilog** are popular logging frameworks for capturing application errors, exceptions, and events. Both libraries offer flexible logging configurations and allow you to log data to multiple outputs, such as files, databases, or external monitoring systems.
   - Use structured logging to capture error details and track the state of the application.
   - Implement error levels (e.g., INFO, ERROR, FATAL) to provide granular insight into system behavior.
2. **Polly for Resilience**: **Polly** is a .NET library that provides resilience and transient-fault-handling capabilities. Polly enables retry logic, circuit

breakers, and timeout handling, making it ideal for implementing fault tolerance in C# applications.

- o Developers can use Polly to define policies for retrying requests to external services, handling timeouts, or isolating faults with circuit breakers.

3. **ASP.NET Core for Fault Tolerance**: **ASP.NET Core** offers built-in support for managing errors and handling fault tolerance in web applications. Features like **middleware for exception handling** and **health checks** can help ensure that services remain operational even in the event of failures.

- o You can configure custom error pages for different environments (development vs. production) and set up global exception handlers to catch and log unhandled exceptions.

4. **Service Fabric and Azure**: **Microsoft Azure Service Fabric** provides an easy way to build and manage distributed, fault-tolerant systems. It enables developers to design highly available services that can automatically recover from failures, scale based on demand, and maintain service integrity across multiple instances and data centers.

Real-World Examples of Reliable Systems

1. **Python - Dropbox**: Dropbox uses Python and leverages various tools for reliability, including **Celery** for background task management and **Kubernetes** for container orchestration. They employ a combination of **replication** and **load balancing** strategies to ensure that their application is available at all times, even during system failures or maintenance periods.

2. **C# - Microsoft Azure**: Azure's cloud platform, which uses **C#** and **.NET**, ensures high availability and fault tolerance through **geo-redundancy** and **failover systems**. Azure uses **Polly** for transient fault handling and **Service Fabric** for managing microservices, ensuring that the system remains reliable and scalable across different regions.

Key Takeaways

- **Reliability** in cross-platform systems is crucial to ensuring that applications function consistently across multiple platforms and environments, offering users a seamless experience.

- **Fault tolerance** and **redundancy** strategies, such as graceful degradation, retry logic, and replication, are essential for ensuring that the application can recover from failures and continue to function properly.

- Both **Python** and **C#** offer powerful tools for ensuring reliability, such as logging frameworks, retry mechanisms, and cloud-based tools for orchestration and failover systems.

Designing reliable systems requires careful planning and a robust approach to fault tolerance, ensuring that your application performs well across platforms and can handle failures gracefully.

CHAPTER 6

AGILE METHODOLOGIES FOR CROSS-PLATFORM DEVELOPMENT

Overview of Agile Development Practices

Agile development is a flexible, iterative approach to software development that emphasizes collaboration, adaptability, and delivering small, functional pieces of a product over time. It contrasts with traditional software development methods, such as the Waterfall model, which follow a linear and sequential process. Agile aims to accommodate changes and feedback throughout the development lifecycle, promoting faster delivery of high-quality software.

The key principles of Agile development are outlined in the **Agile Manifesto**:

1. **Individuals and interactions over processes and tools**: Emphasizes communication and collaboration among team members over relying solely on processes or tools.

2. **Working software over comprehensive documentation**: Prioritizes delivering working software, focusing on functionality rather than exhaustive documentation.

3. **Customer collaboration over contract negotiation**: Engages customers continuously to ensure their needs are met, rather than strictly adhering to initial contracts.

4. **Responding to change over following a plan**: Agile embraces changes in requirements and priorities, even late in development, to deliver better outcomes.

Agile development is structured around **sprints**, typically lasting between 1-4 weeks. Each sprint focuses on delivering a small, functional portion of the application that can be tested, reviewed, and improved upon in subsequent sprints. This iterative approach helps teams adapt to changing requirements, reduces risk, and fosters continuous feedback.

Adapting Agile to Cross-Platform Projects

While Agile methodologies are highly effective in software development, adapting them to cross-platform projects can present unique challenges. Cross-platform development involves creating applications that work seamlessly across multiple platforms (e.g., Windows, macOS, Linux, Android, iOS), which requires careful coordination across different environments and technologies.

Here are several ways Agile can be adapted for cross-platform projects:

1. **Collaborative Cross-Platform Teams**:
   - In traditional Agile, teams may be composed of developers working on the backend, frontend, and other components. In cross-platform projects, however, collaboration between platform-specific teams is even more critical. For instance, developers working on iOS, Android, and web applications must frequently sync up to ensure consistency across platforms.
   - A **cross-functional team** in Agile should include developers, testers, UI/UX designers, and platform-specific experts who can collaborate to ensure the application functions across multiple platforms from the very start.

2. **Unified Backlog for All Platforms**:
   - A unified product backlog should contain tasks and user stories that span across all platforms. It's essential to ensure that cross-platform features and platform-specific requirements are appropriately prioritized.

- o Regularly review and update the backlog during **sprint planning** to include tasks related to adapting features for different platforms (e.g., making sure a new feature works on both iOS and Android).

3. **Cross-Platform Testing and Automation**:

- o Testing is a crucial part of Agile, and it becomes even more important in cross-platform development. Continuous integration (CI) systems should be configured to run tests on multiple platforms automatically.

- o **Automated testing** tools such as **Selenium** (for web) or **Appium** (for mobile) can be integrated into the Agile workflow to ensure that features are tested and validated across all platforms before being released.

- o **Test-Driven Development (TDD)** can be particularly useful in cross-platform projects as it helps ensure consistency across all platforms from the start.

4. **Cross-Platform Frameworks**:

- o Cross-platform frameworks such as **Flutter**, **Xamarin**, **React Native**, and **Qt** can be leveraged in Agile development to reduce complexity and improve speed. These frameworks allow developers to write a single

62

codebase that works across multiple platforms, streamlining the development process.

- o In an Agile context, cross-platform frameworks enable faster prototyping and iteration, as developers don't need to create and maintain separate codebases for each platform.

5. **Frequent Demos and Feedback**:

- o Given that Agile promotes **frequent demos** and **customer feedback**, it's important to incorporate feedback from users across different platforms. Each sprint should end with a review where stakeholders can assess the progress of the application across all platforms and provide feedback for further refinement.
- o This iterative approach ensures that any platform-specific issues are quickly identified and addressed, and users' preferences can be incorporated into the development process.

6. **Agile Planning for Platform-Specific Differences**:

- o Cross-platform projects often involve platform-specific challenges, such as differences in UI design guidelines or hardware capabilities (e.g., Android vs. iOS features). Agile teams need to plan sprints with these differences in mind, ensuring that platform-specific issues are handled in parallel with the core features of the app.

63

○ For example, while an iOS app may use **SwiftUI** for user interface design, the Android version could be designed using **Jetpack Compose**. Agile development should account for these differences while ensuring a consistent user experience across platforms.

Real-World Case Studies of Agile in Action with Python and C#

Case Study 1: Python and Django for Cross-Platform Web Applications

Company: **Spotify**

Challenge: Spotify needed a platform that could scale quickly to serve millions of users while maintaining high-quality, responsive user experiences across web and mobile platforms.

Agile Approach:

- **Cross-functional teams**: Spotify used Agile methodologies to form cross-functional teams that included backend developers, mobile developers, and designers. These teams collaborated closely to ensure the application worked seamlessly across web and mobile platforms.

- **Unified backlog**: Spotify's development teams maintained a unified backlog that prioritized features and fixes for both the web application and mobile versions. Agile practices allowed the team to iterate quickly and deliver improvements on both platforms simultaneously.

- **Continuous Integration (CI) and Testing**: Spotify employed automated testing frameworks to run tests across different platforms, ensuring that features were functional regardless of the platform.

Outcome:

- By using Agile, Spotify was able to continuously roll out new features, fix bugs, and optimize performance without disrupting users. The company maintained a consistent user experience across web and mobile apps, and Agile helped them quickly adapt to changing user needs.

Case Study 2: C# and Xamarin for Cross-Platform Mobile Applications

Company: Alaska Airlines

Challenge: Alaska Airlines needed to build a mobile app that worked on both **Android** and **iOS** platforms. They wanted to deliver a high-performance, user-friendly app while ensuring that features like flight tracking, seat reservations, and mobile check-in were seamlessly integrated.

Agile Approach:

- **Cross-platform team**: Alaska Airlines formed an Agile team that included C# developers familiar with **Xamarin**, a framework for building cross-platform mobile apps. This allowed them to maintain a single codebase for both Android and iOS.
- **Sprint reviews and feedback loops**: The team delivered incremental updates every two weeks, allowing the stakeholders (such as the marketing and customer service teams) to provide feedback and refine the app. This helped ensure that the mobile app met user expectations and functioned properly on both platforms.
- **Automated testing with Appium**: The team used **Appium** for automated testing to ensure that the app performed consistently across Android and iOS.

Outcome:

- By adopting Agile practices, Alaska Airlines was able to launch a cross-platform mobile app on schedule, while continuously improving it based on user feedback. The app's reliability and performance helped improve customer satisfaction and reduced the time spent by passengers on manual check-ins.

Case Study 3: Python and Flask for Cross-Platform Web and Mobile Solutions

Company: **Instagram**

Challenge: Instagram needed to scale its services while maintaining fast load times and responsive features for users on both desktop and mobile platforms.

Agile Approach:

- **Microservices architecture**: Instagram adopted Agile methodologies along with a microservices architecture, which allowed different teams to focus on specific services and quickly iterate on them without affecting the entire platform.
- **Rapid prototyping**: The Python-based backend (using **Flask**) allowed the team to prototype features quickly. Agile practices helped ensure that both the backend services and the front-end UI for web and mobile applications were aligned and could be tested and delivered rapidly.
- **User feedback**: Instagram continuously engaged with users through Agile sprint reviews and focused on

addressing any platform-specific issues in real-time, such as optimizing images for different mobile devices.

Outcome:

- Instagram's success with Agile development allowed them to scale their platform efficiently and deliver frequent updates to both web and mobile apps. The team's ability to respond to user feedback quickly kept the platform highly responsive and competitive in the social media space.

Key Takeaways

- **Agile** methodologies offer flexibility, rapid iteration, and collaboration, making them ideal for cross-platform projects that require frequent updates and seamless user experiences across different platforms.
- **Cross-functional teams** are essential for cross-platform development, as they help ensure consistent functionality across all platforms.
- Real-world case studies, like those of **Spotify**, **Alaska Airlines**, and **Instagram**, demonstrate how Agile practices, combined with tools like **Xamarin**, **Flask**, and automated testing, can streamline cross-platform development and enhance product quality.

By adopting Agile practices, cross-platform development teams can maintain flexibility, improve collaboration, and continuously improve their products, ensuring better outcomes and more efficient development processes.

CHAPTER 7

PERFORMANCE OPTIMIZATION ACROSS PLATFORMS

Techniques to Improve Performance in Cross-Platform Apps

Performance optimization is crucial for delivering a smooth and responsive experience in cross-platform applications. As apps grow in complexity and functionality, ensuring that they perform well across different devices and operating systems becomes more challenging. The key to optimizing performance across platforms lies in identifying and addressing bottlenecks, leveraging platform-specific optimizations, and using best practices to ensure efficiency.

Here are several key techniques to improve performance in cross-platform applications:

1. **Efficient Resource Management**:
    o **Memory Management**: Ensure that your application consumes memory efficiently by releasing resources that are no longer needed. This is particularly important in cross-platform

apps, as each platform (e.g., mobile devices vs. desktop) has its own memory limitations.

- **Lazy Loading**: Load resources only when they are needed, rather than loading everything upfront. This reduces initial load time and allows the app to be responsive early on. For example, images and videos can be loaded only when they come into view, rather than all at once.

2. **Optimizing UI/UX Performance**:

- **Reduce UI Rendering Complexity**: Avoid over-complicated UIs that require extensive redraws or complex animations. Complex UI elements, like large lists or intricate graphics, can negatively impact the performance of cross-platform applications.

- **UI Thread Optimization**: In mobile apps, UI elements should be updated in a separate thread from the main application logic to prevent the app from freezing or becoming unresponsive. Ensure that resource-heavy operations (e.g., database queries or network calls) run in the background.

- **Responsive Layouts**: Use platform-specific design guidelines to ensure that the UI is not only visually appealing but also optimized for the platform's capabilities. For instance, using

71

flexbox for web or **Grid** layouts for mobile can improve rendering performance.

3. **Reducing Computational Load**:
   - **Efficient Algorithms**: Use optimized algorithms and data structures for computationally intensive tasks. For example, if your app handles large amounts of data, use efficient searching and sorting algorithms that minimize CPU usage.
   - **Code Splitting**: Break down large scripts into smaller, manageable pieces that can be loaded dynamically when needed. This technique is particularly useful for web applications built with **JavaScript** frameworks (e.g., **React** or **Angular**), which helps reduce initial loading time.

4. **Minimizing Network Latency**:
   - **Caching**: Use **local caching** mechanisms to reduce the need for repeated network requests. Storing frequently accessed data on the device reduces latency and enhances the user experience.
   - **Compression**: Compress data sent over the network (e.g., images, JSON, or XML files) to minimize the amount of data transferred. This helps in scenarios with limited bandwidth or slow

connections, improving load times and responsiveness.

- o **Asynchronous Requests**: Perform network requests asynchronously to avoid blocking the main thread, ensuring the UI remains responsive during data fetching or syncing tasks.

5. **Cross-Platform Framework Optimization**:

- o Many cross-platform frameworks, such as **Flutter**, **React Native**, **Xamarin**, or **Qt**, come with built-in performance optimization techniques. These frameworks often provide tools to compile down to native code, reducing overhead compared to purely interpreted code. Leveraging these optimizations helps to ensure high performance across platforms.

6. **Offloading Heavy Operations**:

- o **Cloud Computing**: Offload heavy computational tasks, such as image processing, machine learning, or data analysis, to cloud services. This reduces the burden on the client-side app and ensures smoother performance on mobile devices or less powerful platforms.

- o **Edge Computing**: For applications requiring real-time processing, consider using edge computing solutions where computation happens closer to the user, reducing latency.

73

Profiling Tools for Python and C#

To identify performance bottlenecks and areas for optimization, developers must use profiling tools that measure and analyze various aspects of an application's performance. Both Python and C# offer a range of profiling tools to help developers improve the efficiency of their cross-platform applications.

Profiling Tools for Python

1. **cProfile**:
   - ○ **Description**: Python's built-in `cProfile` module is one of the most commonly used profiling tools. It provides a detailed report of function calls, including the time taken by each function and the number of times it was called.
   - ○ **How it helps**: `cProfile` can be used to identify which parts of your Python application consume the most CPU time, helping pinpoint areas for optimization.
   - ○ **Usage**:

```
python

import cProfile
cProfile.run('my_function()')
```

- o **Real-World Application**: In a web application, you can use `cProfile` to analyze the backend code and optimize slow database queries or inefficient logic that may affect performance.

2. **line_profiler**:

- o **Description**: The `line_profiler` tool provides line-by-line profiling, helping you identify performance bottlenecks at the most granular level. It's particularly useful for deep inspection of function-level performance.

- o **How it helps**: It helps track how much time each individual line of code in a function takes to execute, allowing developers to identify slow lines or operations.

- o **Usage**:

```
python

@profile
def my_function():
    # Your code here
```

3. **Py-Spy**:

- o **Description**: `Py-Spy` is a sampling profiler for Python. It runs without modifying the code or requiring a restart of the application, making it

75

ideal for profiling long-running applications in production.

- o **How it helps**: It provides a live snapshot of your Python program's performance, highlighting CPU usage and function calls in real-time.

Profiling Tools for C#

1. **Visual Studio Profiler**:
   - o **Description**: The built-in **Visual Studio Profiler** is a powerful tool for profiling C# applications, particularly for performance bottlenecks related to CPU usage, memory allocation, and thread management.
   - o **How it helps**: It allows you to profile code execution, track memory usage, and find memory leaks or unnecessary allocations. It also supports CPU sampling, which can identify performance hotspots in your application.
   - o **Usage**: Use the **Performance Profiler** within Visual Studio to collect performance data during the execution of your application.

2. **dotTrace**:
   - o **Description**: **dotTrace** by JetBrains is a comprehensive performance profiler for .NET applications. It provides in-depth analysis of CPU

usage, memory allocation, and database query performance.

- o **How it helps**: dotTrace gives detailed performance reports and visualizations to help developers optimize code and reduce execution time or memory consumption.
- o **Usage**: dotTrace can be integrated into your workflow to help you analyze performance metrics at runtime.

3. **BenchmarkDotNet**:

- o **Description**: **BenchmarkDotNet** is a popular library for benchmarking and performance testing in C#. It provides high-precision measurements of how long different parts of your application take to execute.
- o **How it helps**: By benchmarking specific code paths, you can identify bottlenecks in critical sections of your C# application and optimize them for better performance.
- o **Usage**:

```
csharp


[Benchmark]
public void MyFunction()
{
    // Code to benchmark
```

}

Handling Performance Bottlenecks in Real-World Applications

1. **Database Query Optimization**:

- o Performance bottlenecks are often related to database queries, particularly in cross-platform applications that rely on cloud or server-side data. To optimize, ensure that queries are properly indexed and avoid unnecessary joins or expensive operations. Use caching mechanisms to reduce the load on the database for frequently accessed data.

- o In Python, use tools like **SQLAlchemy** to manage database queries and optimize execution. In C#, use **Entity Framework Core** with optimized query practices.

2. **Memory Leaks and Excessive Memory Usage**:

- o In both Python and C#, improper memory management can lead to memory leaks, especially in long-running applications. Use tools like **Py-Spy** or **dotMemory** to identify areas where memory is not being freed appropriately. In C#, implement proper disposal patterns with **IDisposable** to ensure objects are cleaned up after use.

3. **Asynchronous Programming**:

- o For applications that require high concurrency (e.g., handling many users or network requests), implement **asynchronous programming** to prevent blocking operations. In Python, use **asyncio**, and in C#, use **async/await** to ensure non-blocking calls for I/O-bound tasks like database access, file reading, or network requests.

4. **Reducing Latency in Distributed Systems**:
   - o When building distributed systems (e.g., microservices or cloud-based applications), minimize latency by ensuring that services are geographically close to users, optimizing API calls, and reducing the number of round-trip requests.

Key Takeaways

- Optimizing performance across platforms involves efficient resource management, optimizing UI rendering, reducing computational load, and minimizing network latency.
- Profiling tools like **cProfile**, **Visual Studio Profiler**, and **dotTrace** are essential for identifying performance bottlenecks in Python and C# applications.
- Real-world performance bottlenecks often stem from inefficient database queries, memory leaks, or poor

handling of concurrent tasks, all of which can be mitigated with the right techniques and tools.

By leveraging these strategies and profiling tools, you can ensure that your cross-platform applications perform optimally across all target platforms, delivering a smooth and responsive user experience.

CHAPTER 8

EFFECTIVE TESTING STRATEGIES

The Importance of Testing in Cross-Platform Applications

Testing is a critical part of the software development lifecycle, particularly in cross-platform applications where the goal is to ensure consistent functionality and performance across multiple environments (e.g., Windows, macOS, Android, iOS). Cross-platform applications often involve different user interfaces, operating systems, hardware specifications, and network conditions. Ensuring that your application behaves as expected across all these platforms requires thorough testing at multiple levels.

Key reasons why testing is crucial for cross-platform applications:

1. **Platform Variability**: Different platforms may interpret code in unique ways, leading to inconsistencies in behavior. For example, an app might work flawlessly on Android but exhibit rendering issues on iOS. Testing

helps ensure that the application delivers a consistent user experience across all platforms.

2. **User Experience**: A cross-platform app must be smooth, responsive, and intuitive on every platform. Testing helps identify areas where the user experience might suffer due to performance issues, slow load times, or UI inconsistencies.

3. **Integration with Third-Party Services**: Cross-platform apps often rely on third-party libraries, services, or APIs. Testing ensures that the integration works as expected on every platform, even as external services evolve.

4. **Cost and Time Efficiency**: Finding and fixing bugs early in the development process is significantly cheaper than identifying them in production. Comprehensive testing helps prevent costly issues and minimizes time spent troubleshooting after release.

A proper testing strategy for cross-platform applications must include multiple types of tests—**unit tests, integration tests**, and **end-to-end tests**—to ensure that every part of the application functions as expected across platforms.

Unit Tests, Integration Tests, and End-to-End Tests

Each type of test serves a different purpose and helps ensure that different parts of the application are working correctly. Let's look at each test type in more detail:

1. **Unit Tests**

   - **Definition**: Unit tests focus on verifying the smallest parts of an application, typically individual functions or methods. A unit test isolates a single piece of functionality and checks whether it produces the expected output, given a specific input.

   - **Importance**: Unit testing is the first line of defense in catching bugs early. Since unit tests target individual components of the code, they allow developers to identify and fix issues in isolation before they propagate throughout the application.

   - **Example**: In a Python app, you might write a unit test to ensure that a function correctly calculates a user's age based on their birthdate. Similarly, in C#, you can test whether a method correctly handles a specific algorithm.

   - **Best Practices**:
     - Write tests for all critical functions and methods.
     - Ensure that each test is independent (i.e., one test does not rely on another).
     - Use mock objects to simulate interactions with external dependencies (e.g., databases or APIs).

2. **Integration Tests**

- o **Definition**: Integration tests verify that different modules or components of the application work together as expected. These tests check the interactions between various parts of the system (e.g., the frontend and backend, or the database and the application logic).

- o **Importance**: While unit tests are great for checking individual components, integration tests help ensure that those components function correctly when combined. In a cross-platform application, integration tests check that platform-specific components (e.g., native device features) are integrated correctly with the shared codebase.

- o **Example**: For a cross-platform mobile app, an integration test might check whether data from the app's backend is correctly displayed in the UI. In a Python application, this might involve testing how the backend API integrates with the frontend's data-rendering logic.

- o **Best Practices**:
  - Test the most critical interactions between modules and services.
  - Test both local (e.g., database) and external (e.g., third-party API) integrations.

84

- Run integration tests in different environments to ensure consistency.

3. End-to-End Tests

- **Definition**: End-to-end (E2E) tests are designed to verify the application's behavior from the user's perspective. These tests simulate real user interactions and ensure that the app functions as expected from start to finish, covering everything from the UI to the backend.

- **Importance**: E2E testing ensures that the user experience is seamless across all platforms. It also checks whether the application works as a complete system and if all components (e.g., UI, API, database) integrate effectively.

- **Example**: In a cross-platform app, an E2E test might simulate a user logging in, adding an item to the shopping cart, and making a purchase—all while ensuring that the application responds correctly across different platforms.

- **Best Practices**:
  - Simulate real-world user scenarios to ensure the application behaves as expected.
  - Test on actual devices, not just simulators or emulators, to capture platform-specific issues.

- Automate as many E2E tests as possible to reduce manual testing efforts.

Automated Testing Tools for Python and C#

Automated testing tools are essential in cross-platform development. They allow teams to run tests frequently, catch issues early, and ensure that the application works as expected across all platforms. Both Python and C# offer robust automated testing frameworks that make it easier to implement unit tests, integration tests, and E2E tests.

Automated Testing Tools for Python

1. **unittest**:
    - **Description**: Python's built-in `unittest` framework is used for writing unit tests. It provides a rich set of assertion methods and supports organizing tests into test suites for better management.
    - **Usage**: You can write unit tests for individual functions or methods, and the framework will report any test failures.
    - **Example**:

    ```
    python
    ```

```
import unittest
def add(x, y):
    return x + y

class
TestAddFunction(unittest.TestCase):
    def
test_add_positive_numbers(self):
        self.assertEqual(add(2,  3),
5)
```

2. pytest:

- o **Description**: `pytest` is a powerful and flexible testing framework that works well with both unit and integration tests. It has features like test discovery, rich assertions, and easy integration with other testing tools.
- o **Usage**: Use `pytest` for running tests, generating detailed reports, and executing tests across multiple environments.
- o **Example**:

```python
def test_addition():
    assert add(2, 3) == 5
```

3. Selenium:

87

- o **Description**: Selenium is an automated testing tool for web applications. It supports testing across multiple browsers and platforms and allows you to simulate user interactions (clicks, typing, etc.) in a browser.
- o **Usage**: Use Selenium to write E2E tests that ensure the web version of your app behaves as expected.
- o **Example**:

```python
python

from selenium import webdriver
driver = webdriver.Chrome()
driver.get("http://example.com")
assert "Example" in driver.title
driver.quit()
```

4. **Appium**:

- o **Description**: Appium is a cross-platform tool for automating mobile applications (iOS and Android). It enables testing mobile apps through automated E2E tests and supports multiple programming languages, including Python.
- o **Usage**: Automate tests for mobile applications, ensuring the app works as expected on different devices and platforms.
- o **Example**:

88

```python
from appium import webdriver
desired_caps = {
    "platformName": "Android",
    "platformVersion": "9",
    "deviceName": "MyPhone",
    "app": "/path/to/app.apk"
}
driver                              =
webdriver.Remote('http://localhost:
4723/wd/hub', desired_caps)
```

Automated Testing Tools for C#

1. **NUnit**:
   - **Description**: NUnit is a popular testing framework for C# that supports unit and integration testing. It allows developers to write tests, manage test cases, and run them efficiently.
   - **Usage**: Use NUnit for testing individual functions and methods, and integrate it into CI/CD pipelines for automatic test execution.
   - **Example**:

```csharp
using NUnit.Framework;
public class TestClass
```

89

```
{
    [Test]
    public void AddTest()
    {
        Assert.AreEqual(5,      Add(2,
3));
    }
}
```

2. xUnit:

- o **Description**: xUnit is another popular framework for C# testing. It is lightweight, extensible, and designed to handle modern testing needs, including support for parallel test execution.
- o **Usage**: Use xUnit for unit, integration, and E2E testing.
- o **Example**:

```
csharp

public class TestClass
{
    [Fact]
    public void AddTest()
    {
        Assert.Equal(5, Add(2, 3));
    }
}
```

3. **Selenium WebDriver**:

- o **Description**: Selenium WebDriver allows C# developers to automate browser-based testing. It supports testing on all major browsers and operating systems.
- o **Usage**: Write and automate E2E tests for web applications to ensure that user interactions function correctly across different platforms.
- o **Example**:

```csharp
IWebDriver driver = new
ChromeDriver();
driver.Navigate().GoToUrl("http://e
xample.com");
Assert.Contains("Example",
driver.Title);
driver.Quit();
```

4. **Xamarin.UITest**:

- o **Description**: Xamarin.UITest is a testing framework for mobile applications, allowing C# developers to write automated UI tests for Android and iOS apps.
- o **Usage**: Use Xamarin.UITest to ensure that your mobile app functions as expected on both Android and iOS devices.

o **Example**:

```
csharp
```

```csharp
var                  app                =
ConfigureApp.iOS.StartApp();
app.Tap(c => c.Marked("button_id"));
app.Screenshot("ButtonClicked");
```

Key Takeaways

- **Testing** is vital in cross-platform development to ensure consistent behavior across different platforms and provide a seamless user experience.
- **Unit tests**, **integration tests**, and **end-to-end tests** serve different purposes in ensuring that every part of the application functions as expected.
- Both **Python** and **C#** offer a variety of automated testing tools, such as **unittest**, **pytest**, **Selenium**, **NUnit**, and **Xamarin.UITest**, to help streamline the testing process and improve software quality.

By adopting a comprehensive testing strategy and utilizing automated tools, developers can significantly reduce bugs and performance issues, ultimately delivering more reliable and user-friendly cross-platform applications.

CHAPTER 9

CROSS-PLATFORM TOOLS AND FRAMEWORKS

Overview of Popular Cross-Platform Frameworks and Tools

Cross-platform frameworks and tools are designed to simplify the development of applications that work across multiple platforms, such as Windows, macOS, Linux, Android, and iOS, using a single codebase. These frameworks allow developers to avoid the redundancy of writing separate code for each platform, reduce development time, and maintain a consistent user experience. As cross-platform development has gained popularity, several frameworks and tools have emerged, each catering to different types of applications and offering varying levels of support, performance, and flexibility.

Here are some of the most popular cross-platform frameworks and tools:

1. **.NET Core**
   o Developed by Microsoft, .NET Core is a free, open-source, cross-platform framework for

building modern, cloud-based applications. It is particularly well-suited for enterprise-level, server-side, and web applications.

2. Flutter

o Flutter is an open-source UI toolkit developed by Google for creating natively compiled applications for mobile, web, and desktop from a single codebase. It's known for its fast rendering and expressive user interfaces.

3. React Native

o React Native is a popular framework for building mobile applications using JavaScript and React. It allows developers to create apps for Android and iOS using a shared codebase while providing access to native components.

4. Xamarin

o Xamarin is a cross-platform mobile development framework from Microsoft that uses C# and .NET to build Android and iOS apps from a single codebase.

5. Qt

o Qt is a widely-used C++ framework that provides tools for building cross-platform applications for desktop, mobile, and embedded systems. Qt also supports Python bindings, enabling Python developers to use it for desktop apps.

94

6. **Electron**

   o Electron is a framework for building desktop applications using web technologies (HTML, CSS, JavaScript). It is primarily used for creating cross-platform desktop apps that work on Windows, macOS, and Linux.

7. **Apache Cordova (PhoneGap)**

   o Apache Cordova is an open-source mobile development framework that allows developers to build mobile apps using HTML, CSS, and JavaScript. Cordova wraps the app in a native container, allowing it to access device features through JavaScript.

8. **Django & Flask (for Web)**

   o Django and Flask are both popular Python frameworks used for building web applications. Django provides a high-level framework for building full-stack applications, while Flask is a lightweight micro-framework focused on simplicity and flexibility.

These tools and frameworks differ in their approaches, but all aim to simplify the process of building cross-platform applications.

Deep Dive into Frameworks Like .NET Core, Flask, and Django

Let's take a closer look at three of the most commonly used frameworks: **.NET Core**, **Flask**, and **Django**.

1. .NET Core

- **Overview**: .NET Core is an open-source, cross-platform framework developed by Microsoft, designed for building modern web applications, microservices, desktop applications, and more. It's the successor to the older .NET Framework and supports Windows, macOS, and Linux.
- **Key Features**:
  - **Cross-Platform**: Works seamlessly on Windows, macOS, and Linux, allowing developers to write applications that run across platforms without modifying the codebase.
  - **High Performance**: .NET Core is known for its performance, especially in web and cloud applications, thanks to its lightweight architecture.
  - **Compatibility with C#**: Developers can use the C# language, which is known for its strong typing, object-oriented features, and extensive libraries.

96

- o **Integrated Tools**: The framework integrates with powerful tools like **Entity Framework Core** for database management, **ASP.NET Core** for web development, and **Blazor** for building interactive web UIs.

- **Use Cases**:
  - o **Web Development**: ASP.NET Core is used for building high-performance web applications, APIs, and microservices.
  - o **Cloud Applications**: .NET Core is optimized for cloud-based development, making it a good choice for scalable and distributed systems.
  - o **Enterprise Solutions**: The stability, security, and strong tooling make it ideal for large-scale, enterprise-level applications.

- **Real-World Example**: Microsoft's **Azure Cloud** services leverage .NET Core for building scalable cloud applications. Additionally, many enterprise applications in the finance and retail sectors are built using .NET Core due to its performance and robustness.

2. Flask

- **Overview**: Flask is a lightweight, micro web framework for Python. Unlike Django, which is a full-stack framework, Flask provides a minimalistic approach, allowing developers to add only the components they need, making it highly flexible and customizable.

- **Key Features**:
  - o **Minimalistic**: Flask doesn't impose any specific project structure, giving developers full control over how their app is organized.
  - o **Extensible**: Flask's modular approach makes it easy to integrate various components like databases, form handling, authentication, etc., as needed.
  - o **Built-in Development Server**: Flask comes with a built-in server for development, simplifying the testing and debugging process.
  - o **Great for APIs**: Flask is widely used to build RESTful APIs, making it a popular choice for backend services.
- **Use Cases**:
  - o **Web APIs**: Flask is often used to build lightweight APIs that serve as the backend for web or mobile applications.
  - o **Prototyping and Small Projects**: Flask's simplicity makes it ideal for quick prototyping or smaller applications where complexity needs to be kept to a minimum.

- o **Microservices**: Due to its flexibility and modularity, Flask is an excellent choice for building microservices architectures.
- **Real-World Example**: **Netflix** uses Flask for some of its microservices, particularly for APIs that manage content delivery. **Pinterest** also uses Flask for certain backend services due to its simplicity and scalability.

3. Django

- **Overview**: Django is a high-level Python web framework that encourages rapid development and clean, pragmatic design. It provides everything needed for building full-stack applications, including an ORM, authentication system, and an admin interface, making it ideal for large-scale projects.
- **Key Features**:
  - o **Batteries Included**: Django comes with many built-in features such as user authentication, admin panels, form handling, and database migration tools.
  - o **ORM (Object-Relational Mapping)**: Django's ORM allows developers to interact with the database using Python code, abstracting the complexities of raw SQL.

99

- o **Security**: Django has a strong focus on security, with built-in protection against common threats like SQL injection, cross-site scripting (XSS), and cross-site request forgery (CSRF).
- o **Scalability**: Django is designed for scalability, making it suitable for both small and large applications.

- **Use Cases**:
  - o **Full-Stack Web Applications**: Django is widely used to build complex web applications with user authentication, dynamic content, and databases.
  - o **Data-Driven Platforms**: Django is well-suited for building applications that handle a lot of data, such as content management systems (CMS), social media platforms, or e-commerce websites.
  - o **Prototyping**: Due to its "batteries-included" nature, Django is often used for rapid prototyping.

- **Real-World Example**: **Instagram** is built using Django, taking advantage of its scalability and rapid development features to handle millions of users and a large amount of content. **The Washington Post** also uses Django for their website, handling large traffic volumes with ease.

Real-World Examples of Framework Choices for Different Use
Cases

1. **Web Applications**:

- o **Django** is often the go-to choice for developers building large, full-stack web applications. Its built-in components and powerful ORM make it an excellent choice for data-driven platforms like e-commerce stores, social networks, and content management systems.

- o **Flask**, on the other hand, is ideal for developers building lightweight APIs or microservices where flexibility and customization are needed. It's a popular choice for rapid prototyping.

2. **Mobile Applications**:

- o **Xamarin** is often used for cross-platform mobile development when developers want to leverage C# and .NET to build native-like Android and iOS apps. It's especially popular in enterprise environments where existing C# knowledge is a key factor.

- o **React Native** is favored for building mobile applications with a shared codebase in JavaScript, providing fast development cycles and a strong community support base.

3. **Cloud Services**:

o **.NET Core** is ideal for cloud-based applications, especially when using **Microsoft Azure**. It supports microservices, APIs, and serverless computing, making it a great choice for scalable and cloud-native solutions.

o **Flask** is also used in cloud environments for lightweight backend services, often combined with cloud-native tools like **AWS Lambda** or **Google Cloud Functions** to build serverless applications.

4. **Cross-Platform Desktop Applications**:

o **Qt** is often chosen for building cross-platform desktop applications, particularly when performance and control over low-level components are important. It's widely used in industries that require custom graphical interfaces, like CAD software.

o **Electron** is another popular choice for building cross-platform desktop apps using web technologies. It's often used by developers familiar with web technologies (HTML, CSS, JavaScript) to quickly create desktop apps that work across Windows, macOS, and Linux.

Key Takeaways

- **Cross-platform frameworks** allow developers to build applications that work across multiple platforms, reducing development time and ensuring consistency.
- Frameworks like **.NET Core**, **Flask**, and **Django** cater to different use cases, with .NET Core being ideal for enterprise solutions, Flask excelling at lightweight APIs, and Django being suited for full-stack applications.
- Real-world examples show how different frameworks are chosen based on the needs of the project, such as using Django for data-driven platforms and Xamarin for cross-platform mobile development.

By selecting the right framework and tool for your project's needs, you can significantly improve the development process, optimize performance, and ensure that your application works seamlessly across all target platforms.

CHAPTER 10

CLOUD INTEGRATION IN CROSS-PLATFORM DEVELOPMENT

The Role of Cloud Services in Cross-Platform Architecture

Cloud services play a crucial role in modern cross-platform development by providing scalable, reliable, and flexible resources for deploying, managing, and maintaining applications. As cross-platform apps need to function seamlessly across different environments (e.g., mobile, desktop, and web), cloud services help centralize data storage, facilitate real-time synchronization, manage authentication, and handle large-scale computing tasks that would otherwise overwhelm local resources.

Here are the key roles cloud services play in cross-platform architecture:

1. **Centralized Data Management**:
   - Cross-platform apps often need to synchronize data across different devices and platforms. Cloud storage solutions (e.g., Amazon S3, Google Cloud Storage, or Azure Blob Storage)

104

allow seamless data storage and access for users, regardless of whether they are on mobile, desktop, or web.

2. **Scalability**:

   o   As the number of users grows, cross-platform applications need to scale efficiently. Cloud platforms offer scalable compute resources, such as virtual machines (VMs), serverless functions, and containers, that can automatically scale up or down based on demand. This flexibility ensures that performance is maintained even as the user base expands.

3. **Real-Time Communication**:

   o   Cloud services enable real-time updates and communication between users on different platforms. For instance, **Firebase** offers real-time databases that sync data instantly between clients, providing a seamless experience for users across platforms (such as messaging apps or collaborative tools).

4. **Security and Authentication**:

   o   Cloud platforms provide powerful tools for managing user authentication and authorization across platforms. **OAuth** or **JWT** tokens, combined with cloud authentication services like **Firebase Authentication** or **Azure Active**

Directory, simplify cross-platform user management and ensure that user data is kept secure.

5. **CI/CD Pipelines**:

   o Cloud-based Continuous Integration/Continuous Deployment (CI/CD) tools automate testing, building, and deployment processes for cross-platform apps. This ensures that code changes are tested, integrated, and deployed efficiently across all platforms, providing developers with an automated way to manage the entire development lifecycle.

6. **Backend-as-a-Service (BaaS)**:

   o Cloud platforms like **Firebase** and **AWS Amplify** offer Backend-as-a-Service solutions, allowing developers to offload server-side logic and reduce the need for custom backend infrastructure. This allows faster development of cross-platform apps, as developers can focus on the front-end without worrying about setting up and maintaining backend servers.

Leveraging Cloud Platforms (AWS, Azure, Google Cloud)

Major cloud platforms offer various services that enable cross-platform app development, each with its own set of strengths and capabilities. Let's explore the three most widely used cloud providers and how they can be leveraged for cross-platform development:

1. Amazon Web Services (AWS)

AWS is one of the most popular cloud platforms, providing a broad range of services for computing, storage, networking, and machine learning. AWS is widely used for both large and small-scale cross-platform applications due to its scalability, reliability, and extensive ecosystem.

- **AWS Services for Cross-Platform Development**:
    - o **AWS Lambda**: Serverless computing that lets you run code without provisioning or managing servers. Perfect for handling event-driven workloads or APIs that serve your cross-platform apps.
    - o **Amazon S3**: Object storage for storing and retrieving data, such as images, videos, and documents, across multiple platforms. S3 is highly durable and integrates well with other AWS services.
    - o **Amazon API Gateway**: Enables you to build and manage APIs that connect your cross-platform

app with cloud resources, ensuring seamless communication across platforms.

- o **AWS Amplify**: A development platform that simplifies backend setup for cross-platform apps. It provides tools for user authentication, APIs, storage, and real-time data synchronization.

- o **AWS Elastic Beanstalk**: A Platform-as-a-Service (PaaS) solution for deploying web applications, where developers can simply upload their code, and Elastic Beanstalk takes care of provisioning and scaling the infrastructure.

- **Real-World Example**: Many high-traffic applications like **Netflix** and **Airbnb** use AWS to manage user data, videos, and images, ensuring smooth performance across devices.

2. Microsoft Azure

Azure is a cloud computing platform by Microsoft, providing comprehensive services for building, deploying, and managing cross-platform applications. Azure is particularly strong in integrating with **Microsoft technologies** (e.g., .NET Core, C#), making it an excellent choice for developers using these tools for cross-platform development.

- **Azure Services for Cross-Platform Development**:
  - ○ **Azure App Services**: PaaS solution for building and hosting web apps, APIs, and mobile backends. It supports multiple programming languages, including Python and C#, and can scale automatically based on traffic.
  - ○ **Azure Functions**: Serverless computing for executing code in response to triggers (e.g., HTTP requests, database changes) without managing servers. Ideal for building scalable microservices that integrate with your cross-platform app.
  - ○ **Azure Storage**: Blob Storage, Queue Storage, and File Storage services that provide centralized data storage, accessible by your cross-platform app.
  - ○ **Azure Active Directory (Azure AD)**: Cloud-based identity and access management service for integrating authentication across multiple platforms. This is ideal for securing user data and enabling single sign-on (SSO) for your app users.
  - ○ **Azure DevOps**: Provides CI/CD pipelines, version control, and project management tools, helping automate deployment and testing for cross-platform applications.

109

- **Real-World Example**: **Slack** uses **Azure** to power its cross-platform messaging system, ensuring fast data synchronization and secure, scalable infrastructure for users across devices.

3. Google Cloud Platform (GCP)

Google Cloud offers a wide range of cloud services optimized for data storage, machine learning, analytics, and application hosting. GCP is an excellent choice for cross-platform developers looking for AI-powered services and high-performance computing resources.

- **GCP Services for Cross-Platform Development**:
  - **Firebase**: Google's Backend-as-a-Service platform, which is particularly useful for mobile applications. Firebase offers authentication, real-time databases, push notifications, and cloud functions, making it ideal for building scalable cross-platform apps.
  - **Google Cloud Storage**: A fully managed object storage service that scales automatically to meet the needs of cross-platform applications. Perfect for handling user data, media files, and backups.
  - **Google Cloud Functions**: Serverless functions that execute in response to events, such as HTTP

requests or changes in Cloud Storage, making it easy to build event-driven applications.

- **Google Kubernetes Engine (GKE)**: Manages containerized applications across multiple platforms. GKE helps automate the deployment, scaling, and operation of applications, ensuring that cross-platform apps perform efficiently at scale.

- **BigQuery**: A fully-managed data warehouse solution that allows you to store and analyze large volumes of data. Useful for apps that require data analytics and real-time insights, such as e-commerce platforms or social networks.

- **Real-World Example**: **Snapchat** uses **Google Cloud** services, particularly **Firebase** for real-time database synchronization and user authentication, ensuring seamless performance across mobile devices.

Building and Deploying Cross-Platform Apps on the Cloud

Building and deploying cross-platform apps in the cloud involves several key steps, including backend development, cloud service integration, deployment, and scaling. Here's an overview of the process:

1. **Backend Development**:
    - o Choose the appropriate cloud services (e.g., AWS Lambda, Google Cloud Functions, or Azure Functions) for building backend logic. These services enable you to write scalable, event-driven functions that interact with your app.
    - o Use cloud databases (e.g., **AWS DynamoDB, Azure Cosmos DB**, or **Google Firestore**) for storing and managing data, ensuring data consistency and availability across platforms.
    - o Integrate authentication systems using cloud-based identity providers (e.g., **AWS Cognito, Firebase Authentication, Azure AD**) to secure user data.

2. **Cloud Storage and File Management**:
    - o Store media and application data in cloud storage services (e.g., **Amazon S3, Google Cloud Storage**, or **Azure Blob Storage**) to make the data accessible across different platforms and devices.
    - o Implement cloud functions to trigger actions based on file uploads or database changes, such as notifying users when new content is available.

3. **CI/CD Pipelines**:
    - o Set up automated testing and deployment pipelines using cloud-native tools like **AWS**

CodePipeline, Azure DevOps, or **Google Cloud Build**. These tools automatically deploy your cross-platform app to production environments after successful tests.

o Integrate testing tools into the CI/CD pipeline to ensure that changes are validated across platforms before being deployed.

4. **Scalability and Load Balancing**:

o Ensure that your app can handle traffic spikes by leveraging auto-scaling features in cloud platforms like **AWS Elastic Beanstalk, Azure App Services**, or **Google App Engine**.

o Use cloud load balancers to distribute traffic efficiently across servers and ensure high availability.

5. **Monitoring and Analytics**:

o Use cloud-native monitoring tools like **Amazon CloudWatch, Azure Monitor**, or **Google Cloud Operations** to track the performance of your application, monitor resource usage, and receive alerts for any issues.

o Analyze user interactions and app performance using cloud analytics tools such as **Google Analytics, AWS QuickSight**, or **Azure Analytics** to optimize the user experience.

Key Takeaways

- **Cloud services** are integral to building scalable, reliable, and flexible cross-platform applications. They provide essential infrastructure for backend logic, data storage, user authentication, and application deployment.

- **AWS**, **Azure**, and **Google Cloud** offer powerful tools that streamline cloud integration, from serverless computing to CI/CD pipelines to data analytics, making them indispensable for modern cross-platform development.

- Building and deploying cross-platform apps on the cloud involves backend development, cloud storage integration, CI/CD pipelines, and scaling to handle user demands across multiple platforms.

By leveraging the right cloud services, developers can ensure their cross-platform apps are scalable, secure, and optimized for performance, providing a seamless experience for users on any device.

CHAPTER 11

MANAGING DATA IN CROSS-PLATFORM APPLICATIONS

Data Consistency, Storage, and Retrieval Across Platforms

Data consistency, storage, and retrieval are critical aspects of cross-platform development. When an application needs to function across multiple platforms (e.g., mobile, desktop, and web), it must ensure that data is consistent across all devices. This consistency is essential for maintaining a seamless user experience and preventing errors caused by data discrepancies.

1. **Data Consistency**:
   - Data consistency means that the same data is available across all platforms at any given time, ensuring that users get an accurate and up-to-date version of the application, whether they access it on a desktop, mobile device, or web browser.
   - In a cross-platform application, consistency is maintained by implementing strong data synchronization and conflict resolution mechanisms. This ensures that when users update

data on one platform, it is reflected across all other platforms without causing conflicts.

2. **Storage**:

   o **Local Storage**: Cross-platform apps often store data locally on the user's device to provide offline access. This data can then be synchronized with the cloud when a network connection is available. Local storage solutions vary based on the platform (e.g., SQLite, IndexedDB, local storage, or mobile databases like Realm).

   o **Cloud Storage**: For cloud-based applications, data is stored on cloud servers, allowing users to access it from any platform. Services like **Amazon S3**, **Google Cloud Storage**, and **Azure Blob Storage** offer scalable storage solutions.

3. **Retrieval**:

   o Efficient retrieval of data is essential for providing a fast and responsive user experience, especially in cross-platform apps where data is accessed from various devices. The choice of database and retrieval method impacts the performance of your app.

   o Using caching mechanisms like **Redis** (for server-side data) or **local storage caches** on mobile devices ensures that frequently accessed

116

data is retrieved quickly, minimizing latency and improving overall performance.

Databases and ORM Solutions for Python and C#

Databases and Object-Relational Mapping (ORM) solutions are crucial when building cross-platform applications that require data storage and management. ORMs provide a way to interact with databases using object-oriented principles, making it easier to perform CRUD (Create, Read, Update, Delete) operations.

Databases for Cross-Platform Applications

1. **Relational Databases**:
   o **PostgreSQL**, **MySQL**, and **SQLite** are popular relational databases used in cross-platform development. These databases organize data into tables and support SQL queries to interact with the data.
   o Relational databases are ideal for applications that need strong data integrity and structured relationships between data entities.

2. **NoSQL Databases**:
   o **MongoDB**, **CouchDB**, and **Firebase Realtime Database** are popular NoSQL databases used for

unstructured data, such as documents or key-value pairs.

o NoSQL databases are ideal for apps that require flexibility, high scalability, and the ability to store various types of data (e.g., user profiles, social media posts, etc.).

ORM Solutions for Python and C#

1. **Python ORM Solutions**:
   o **SQLAlchemy**:
      - SQLAlchemy is one of the most popular ORM libraries for Python, offering support for both relational databases (like PostgreSQL, MySQL) and NoSQL solutions. It provides a set of high-level API tools for working with databases, simplifying queries and database interaction.
      - **Key Features**: SQLAlchemy's **Object-Relational Mapping** allows developers to interact with the database using Python objects, abstracting the need to write raw SQL.
      - **Usage**:

```python
```

```python
from sqlalchemy import
create_engine, Column,
Integer, String
from
sqlalchemy.ext.declarative
import declarative_base
from sqlalchemy.orm import
sessionmaker

Base = declarative_base()

class User(Base):
    __tablename__ = 'users'
    id = Column(Integer,
primary_key=True)
    name = Column(String)
    age = Column(Integer)

engine =
create_engine('sqlite:///user
s.db')
Base.metadata.create_all(engi
ne)

Session =
sessionmaker(bind=engine)
session = Session()
```

119

```
new_user = User(name='Alice',
age=25)
session.add(new_user)
session.commit()
```

o **Django ORM**:

  ▪ Django provides an ORM that is tightly integrated with the Django web framework. It's ideal for developers who are building full-stack web applications with a structured approach to databases.

  ▪ **Key Features**: Django ORM supports multiple relational databases and simplifies database migrations, data validation, and querying.

  ▪ **Usage**: Django uses model classes that represent database tables. The ORM automatically translates queries into SQL.

```python
from django.db import models

class User(models.Model):
    name                   =
models.CharField(max_length=1
00)
```

120

```
age                    =
models.IntegerField()

# Querying
users = User.objects.all()
```

2. C# ORM Solutions:

o Entity Framework Core (EF Core):

- EF Core is the primary ORM framework for .NET developers, allowing them to interact with relational databases using C# objects. It's cross-platform, working on Windows, macOS, and Linux.

- **Key Features**: EF Core provides robust support for querying, tracking changes, and managing database migrations. It integrates seamlessly with **ASP.NET Core** for building web APIs.

- **Usage**:

```csharp
public class User
{
    public int Id { get; set;
}
    public string Name { get;
set; }
```

121

```
        public int Age { get; set;
}
}

public class AppDbContext :
DbContext
{
    public DbSet<User> Users {
get; set; }
}

// Usage in the application
using (var context = new
AppDbContext())
{
    var user = new User { Name
= "Alice", Age = 25 };
    context.Users.Add(user);
    context.SaveChanges();
}
```

- o **Dapper**:
  - Dapper is a lightweight ORM that works well with C# for applications that require fast database access. Unlike Entity Framework, Dapper doesn't provide automatic tracking of entity changes, so developers need to handle that manually.

122

- **Key Features**: Dapper is extremely fast and lightweight, making it a great choice for performance-sensitive applications where raw SQL queries are required but with some object-mapping functionality.

Real-World Examples of Data Synchronization and Integration

1. **Syncing Data in Mobile Apps**:
   o **Firebase Realtime Database** is a common solution for syncing data in real-time across devices, especially in mobile applications. For instance, in a chat application, whenever one user sends a message, the message is immediately available to all other users on all platforms.
   o **Example**: A cross-platform mobile app built with **React Native** and **Firebase** allows users to see chat messages in real-time, with the Firebase Realtime Database ensuring that updates are reflected instantly across Android and iOS devices.

2. **Cross-Platform eCommerce Application**:
   o An eCommerce platform might use **SQLAlchemy** or **Django ORM** for data management, with products, orders, and customer information stored in a relational database. The platform must ensure that user purchases made on

the mobile app are synchronized with the website and backend systems.

- o **Example**: A user adds items to their shopping cart on the mobile app, and the data is saved in the cloud (e.g., **Amazon RDS** or **Google Cloud SQL**). When they log in from another device, the cart information is synced and available, thanks to the backend database and APIs that support data synchronization across platforms.

3. **Real-Time Collaboration Apps**:

- o In real-time collaboration applications, such as those for document editing or project management, data synchronization is vital to ensure all users see the most current version of a document, regardless of the platform they are using.
- o **Example**: A cross-platform project management tool, using **MongoDB** for storing task data and **WebSockets** for real-time communication, ensures that when a user updates a task, the changes are reflected instantly across all devices and platforms.

4. **Cloud-Based Storage and Syncing**:

- o Many cross-platform applications rely on cloud services like **AWS S3** or **Google Cloud Storage** for file storage and synchronization. For example, a photo-sharing app stores images in the cloud and synchronizes them across devices.

- o **Example**: A user uploads a photo on their mobile device, and the image is instantly available in their cloud storage (e.g., **Amazon S3**). On another device, the user accesses the same cloud storage, ensuring consistent access to their images from anywhere.

Key Takeaways

- **Data consistency**, storage, and retrieval across platforms are essential for cross-platform applications to function seamlessly. Cloud storage and local databases help centralize and synchronize data across platforms.
- **ORM solutions** like **SQLAlchemy**, **Django ORM**, and **Entity Framework Core** simplify database interactions and provide an object-oriented approach to managing data in cross-platform applications.
- **Data synchronization and integration** are crucial for ensuring that data is up-to-date across different platforms and devices. Solutions like **Firebase**, **AWS**, and **Google Cloud** provide robust tools for handling real-time synchronization and cloud storage.

By using the right database, ORM, and synchronization solutions, developers can build efficient, scalable cross-platform applications that ensure consistent and fast data access across all platforms.

CHAPTER 12

SECURITY IN CROSS-PLATFORM SYSTEMS

Understanding Security Risks in Cross-Platform Development

Cross-platform development offers numerous benefits, such as reduced development time and cost. However, it also introduces unique security challenges that developers must address to protect sensitive data and ensure the integrity of their applications. Some of the key security risks in cross-platform systems include:

1. **Platform-Specific Vulnerabilities**:
   o Each platform (e.g., Windows, macOS, iOS, Android) has its own set of vulnerabilities and security issues. These can range from weaknesses in native APIs to differences in how platforms handle user data and permissions. Cross-platform apps must be tested for these vulnerabilities on all platforms they target.

2. **Inconsistent Encryption and Data Handling**:
   o Different platforms might handle encryption and data storage differently. For instance, a cross-

platform app might use weak or inconsistent encryption when storing sensitive information on a mobile device or cloud. This can leave data exposed to attackers.

3. **Authentication and Authorization Issues**:
   - o Ensuring that authentication and authorization processes work seamlessly across platforms can be challenging. Weak authentication schemes, such as poor password management or insecure third-party login systems, can be exploited to gain unauthorized access to user accounts.

4. **API Security**:
   - o Cross-platform applications often rely on APIs to communicate between platforms or with backend services. APIs can become targets for attackers if they are not secured properly. Issues like lack of input validation, broken authentication, and improper access control can make APIs vulnerable.

5. **Cross-Site Scripting (XSS) and Cross-Site Request Forgery (CSRF)**:
   - o These are common web application vulnerabilities that also affect cross-platform apps. XSS involves injecting malicious scripts into web pages, while CSRF forces a user's

browser to perform unwanted actions on an authenticated website.

6. **Data Leaks**:

    o   Data leaks can occur when sensitive information, such as user credentials, financial information, or personal data, is inadvertently exposed or not properly protected during transmission or storage.

Best Practices for Securing Python and C# Applications

Securing cross-platform applications requires implementing strong security practices at every stage of development. Whether using Python, C#, or any other language, security should be a top priority.

1. Secure Authentication and Authorization

- **Use OAuth 2.0 or OpenID Connect**: Implement OAuth 2.0 or OpenID Connect for secure authentication and authorization. These modern standards ensure that sensitive information like passwords is never exposed or stored inappropriately.

- **Python**: Libraries like **Authlib** or **Flask-OAuthlib** provide OAuth 2.0 implementation for Python applications.
- **C#**: Use **ASP.NET Core Identity** or **Microsoft Identity** for building secure authentication systems in C#.

- **Multi-Factor Authentication (MFA)**: Require multi-factor authentication (MFA) to add an extra layer of security. Even if a user's password is compromised, MFA ensures that an attacker cannot easily gain access to sensitive data.

- **JWT Tokens for Stateless Authentication**: JSON Web Tokens (JWT) are commonly used for securely transmitting information between a server and a client in a stateless manner. Both Python and C# provide libraries to work with JWT tokens for managing secure sessions.
  - **Python**: Use **PyJWT** to create and verify JWT tokens.
  - **C#**: Use **System.IdentityModel.Tokens.Jwt** for handling JWT tokens in ASP.NET applications.

2. Encryption and Secure Data Handling

- **Use Strong Encryption**: Always encrypt sensitive data, both in transit and at rest. Implement **AES-256** for data encryption and ensure that SSL/TLS is used for secure communication between client and server.

- o **Python**: Use libraries like **cryptography** or **PyCryptodome** to implement encryption.
- o **C#**: Use the **System.Security.Cryptography** namespace in C# for AES encryption and decryption.

- **Store Sensitive Data Securely**: When storing sensitive information, such as passwords or API keys, use secure storage mechanisms provided by the platform. For example, mobile apps can use secure storage APIs like **iOS Keychain** or **Android Keystore** to store sensitive data.

- **Secure API Communication**: Ensure all API communication is encrypted using HTTPS, and never transmit sensitive data over unsecured channels. Implement API security best practices, such as input validation, rate limiting, and proper access control.

- o **Python**: Use **Flask-Security** or **Django Rest Framework** to secure APIs.
- o **C#**: Use **ASP.NET Core** middleware like **Authorization** and **Authentication** for securing APIs.

3. Input Validation and Protection Against Injection Attacks

- **SQL Injection Prevention**: SQL injection is one of the most common attacks. Use parameterized queries or ORM frameworks that prevent direct injection into SQL queries.
  - o **Python**: Use **SQLAlchemy** for ORM-based queries, which automatically protects against SQL injection.
  - o **C#**: Use **Entity Framework** to handle database queries, as it automatically protects against SQL injection attacks by using parameterized queries.

- **Cross-Site Scripting (XSS) Protection**: Sanitize user input to avoid XSS attacks, where malicious scripts are injected into the application's content.
  - o **Python**: Use libraries like **Bleach** to sanitize HTML content and prevent script injections.
  - o **C#**: In ASP.NET, use **AntiXSS** and **HtmlEncode** to sanitize user input and prevent XSS attacks.

- **Cross-Site Request Forgery (CSRF) Protection**: CSRF attacks occur when unauthorized actions are performed on behalf of an authenticated user. Implement **CSRF tokens** to prevent this type of attack.
  - o **Python**: **Django** includes built-in CSRF protection.

- **C#**: In **ASP.NET Core**, use the built-in **[ValidateAntiForgeryToken]** attribute to protect against CSRF attacks.

4. Secure Development Practices

- **Least Privilege Principle**: Always follow the principle of least privilege by giving users and services the minimum permissions necessary to perform their tasks. This limits the potential damage in case of a security breach.

- **Regular Patching and Updates**: Ensure that all software dependencies, libraries, and frameworks are regularly updated to patch any known security vulnerabilities. Use dependency management tools to automate this process.

- **Secure Development Lifecycle (SDLC)**: Integrate security practices throughout the software development lifecycle. Perform code reviews, security testing (e.g., static code analysis), and regular vulnerability assessments to identify potential weaknesses.

Real-World Examples of Securing Sensitive Data

1. **Securing Payments in E-commerce Applications**:

- o Payment data is highly sensitive and must be protected at all costs. A cross-platform e-commerce application uses encryption and tokenization to protect credit card information during transactions.

- o **Example**: An e-commerce app built with **React Native** and **AWS** might integrate **AWS KMS (Key Management Service)** to securely manage encryption keys and encrypt sensitive payment data. The app also ensures PCI-DSS compliance by using **Stripe** for payment processing, which handles the security of sensitive payment data.

2. **Social Media Applications and User Privacy**:

- o Social media applications store vast amounts of sensitive data, including personal messages, user posts, and location information. Implementing encryption both in transit (using SSL/TLS) and at rest (using AES encryption) ensures that this data is protected from unauthorized access.

- o **Example**: A social media app built with **Flask** and **Firebase** ensures that user messages are encrypted before being stored in the database. **Firebase Authentication** is used for secure user sign-ins, and **Firestore** stores user data securely using rules that restrict access based on user identity.

134

3. **Health Apps and HIPAA Compliance**:
    o   Health apps must ensure that sensitive medical information is stored and transmitted securely to comply with regulations such as HIPAA (Health Insurance Portability and Accountability Act).
    o   **Example**: A cross-platform health application built using **Xamarin** stores user health data in a secure cloud environment like **Azure**, where data is encrypted at rest and transmitted securely over HTTPS. The app uses **Azure Active Directory** for secure authentication, ensuring only authorized users can access medical data.

4. **Cloud-Based File Storage and Sharing**:
    o   File-sharing apps often handle sensitive files like documents, images, and videos. Securing these files involves using strong encryption and access control.
    o   **Example**: An enterprise file-sharing system built with **ASP.NET Core** and **Azure Blob Storage** uses encryption to protect data at rest and **Azure AD** for controlling user access. Files are encrypted with AES-256 before being uploaded to **Azure Blob Storage**, ensuring secure access.

Key Takeaways

- **Security risks** in cross-platform development include platform-specific vulnerabilities, inconsistent data handling, insecure authentication, and API weaknesses.
- **Best practices** for securing cross-platform applications include using strong authentication methods (e.g., OAuth 2.0, MFA), encrypting sensitive data, validating user input, and protecting against common attacks like SQL injection and XSS.
- **Real-world examples** show how various industries—e-commerce, social media, healthcare, and file sharing—use encryption, secure APIs, and access control to protect sensitive data across multiple platforms.

By following these best practices and understanding the security challenges of cross-platform development, you can create applications that not only deliver a great user experience but also ensure the safety and privacy of sensitive user data.

CHAPTER 13

CONTINUOUS INTEGRATION AND CONTINUOUS DEPLOYMENT (CI/CD)

Overview of CI/CD Practices in Cross-Platform Development

Continuous Integration (CI) and Continuous Deployment (CD) are modern development practices designed to improve the software development lifecycle by automating the process of integrating and deploying code. These practices are particularly valuable in cross-platform development, where managing multiple platforms and environments can be complex. By implementing CI/CD, teams can streamline development, reduce errors, and ensure that applications remain consistent across all platforms.

Continuous Integration (CI) refers to the practice of automatically integrating code changes into a shared repository multiple times a day. Each integration is verified by an automated build and testing process, which ensures that the new code doesn't break existing functionality.

Continuous Deployment (CD) takes this process a step further by automatically deploying code to production as soon as it passes the integration and testing stages. This ensures that updates are delivered quickly and consistently to users, without manual intervention.

Benefits of CI/CD in Cross-Platform Development:

1. **Faster Development**: CI/CD allows teams to deliver features and bug fixes faster by automating the build, test, and deployment processes.

2. **Consistency Across Platforms**: CI/CD ensures that the application is built and deployed in the same way across all platforms (e.g., web, mobile, and desktop), reducing platform-specific issues.

3. **Increased Reliability**: By integrating code frequently and running automated tests, CI/CD helps catch bugs early, ensuring that the code remains stable.

4. **Improved Collaboration**: CI/CD fosters better communication and collaboration between teams, as developers can focus on writing code without worrying about the deployment process.

5. **Faster Feedback**: Automated tests provide immediate feedback on whether changes are working as expected, enabling quick corrections before code is deployed.

Implementing CI/CD Pipelines with Python and C#

To implement CI/CD for cross-platform applications, developers typically use a CI/CD tool (e.g., **Jenkins**, **GitLab CI**, **CircleCI**, **Azure DevOps**) and configure a series of steps or pipelines that define the process from code integration to deployment.

CI/CD Pipeline for Python Applications

1. **Code Repository**: Developers push their code changes to a version control system (e.g., **GitHub**, **GitLab**). The CI tool monitors the repository for changes.
2. **Build and Test**:
   - **Build**: The CI tool triggers the build process, where the application is compiled or packaged. For Python, this may involve creating a **virtual environment** and installing dependencies from `requirements.txt`.
   - **Test**: Automated tests (e.g., unit tests, integration tests) are run to ensure the new changes don't break the application. Tools like **pytest** or **unittest** are commonly used in Python.
   - **Code Quality**: Tools like **flake8** or **black** are used to enforce coding standards and check for potential issues.

3. **Artifact Creation**: If the tests pass, an artifact (e.g., a Python package or a Docker image) is created and stored in a repository for deployment.

4. **Deployment**: The artifact is automatically deployed to staging or production environments. For cross-platform applications, this may involve deploying to various platforms (e.g., web, iOS, Android).

Example CI/CD Pipeline Configuration (GitLab CI for Python):

```yaml
stages:
  - test
  - deploy

test:
  stage: test
  script:
    - pip install -r requirements.txt
    - pytest tests/

deploy:
  stage: deploy
  script:
    - docker build -t myapp .
    - docker push myapp:latest
    - deploy-to-server.sh
```

140

CI/CD Pipeline for C# Applications

1. **Code Repository**: Developers push code changes to a **Git** repository, and the CI tool (e.g., **Azure DevOps**, **GitHub Actions**) listens for changes.

2. **Build and Test**:
   - **Build**: The C# application is built using **MSBuild** or **dotnet build**, and dependencies are restored using **NuGet**.
   - **Test**: The pipeline runs automated unit tests and integration tests using **NUnit**, **xUnit**, or **MSTest**.
   - **Static Code Analysis**: Tools like **SonarQube** can be used to check code quality and identify security vulnerabilities.

3. **Artifact Creation**: The build artifacts (e.g., **DLLs** or **EXEs**) are packaged and stored in an artifact repository, such as **Azure Artifacts** or **GitHub Packages**.

4. **Deployment**: The deployment stage deploys the app to staging or production environments. This could involve deploying to **Azure App Services**, **AWS Elastic Beanstalk**, or **Kubernetes clusters**.

Example CI/CD Pipeline Configuration (Azure DevOps for C#):

yaml

```
trigger:
- main

pool:
  vmImage: 'windows-latest'

steps:
- task: UseDotNet@2
  inputs:
    packageType: 'sdk'
    version: '5.x'
    installationPath:
$(Agent.ToolsDirectory)/dotnet

- task: DotNetCoreCLI@2
  inputs:
    command: 'restore'
    projects: '**/*.csproj'

- task: DotNetCoreCLI@2
  inputs:
    command: 'build'
    projects: '**/*.csproj'

- task: DotNetCoreCLI@2
  inputs:
    command: 'test'
    projects: '**/*.csproj'
```

```
- task: DotNetCoreCLI@2
  inputs:
    command: 'publish'
    publishWebProjects: true
    projects: '**/*.csproj'
    arguments: '--configuration Release --output
$(Build.ArtifactStagingDirectory)'

- task: AzureWebApp@1
  inputs:
    azureSubscription: '<Azure_Subscription>'
    appName: '<App_Name>'
    package:
'$(Build.ArtifactStagingDirectory)/**/*.zip'
```

Key Stages of CI/CD Pipelines for Both Python and C#

1. **Code Commit**: Developers commit code to a shared repository (e.g., **GitHub**, **GitLab**, **Bitbucket**), triggering the CI pipeline.

2. **Build Stage**: Code is compiled (for C#) or packaged (for Python). Dependencies are installed and the application is built into deployable artifacts.

3. **Test Stage**: Automated tests are run, ensuring that new code does not introduce regressions or break existing functionality.

4. **Deploy Stage**: After passing the tests, the application is deployed to staging or production environments. Deployment can involve cloud platforms (e.g., **AWS**,

Azure, **Google Cloud**) or containerized environments (e.g., **Docker, Kubernetes**).

5. **Monitoring**: Continuous monitoring tools (e.g., **Datadog**, **Prometheus**) are used to track the performance and health of the application after deployment.

Real-Life Examples of Automated Deployment

1. E-Commerce Website (Python + Django)

- o An e-commerce website built using **Django** with a Python backend and a **React** frontend uses CI/CD to automate the deployment process. Developers push code to a GitHub repository, and **GitHub Actions** runs the pipeline, which builds the project, runs tests, and deploys the application to an **AWS EC2 instance**.
- o **Deployment Process**:
  1. Code is pushed to GitHub.
  2. **GitHub Actions** triggers the pipeline.
  3. **Docker** images are built for the backend and frontend.
  4. The images are pushed to **AWS ECR (Elastic Container Registry)**.
  5. The app is deployed to **AWS ECS (Elastic Container Service)**, and traffic is routed via **AWS ALB (Application Load Balancer)**.

2. Cross-Platform Mobile App (C# + Xamarin)

- A mobile app built using **Xamarin** is deployed using **Azure DevOps**. The app is cross-platform, targeting both **Android** and **iOS**. The CI/CD pipeline is triggered by code pushes to **Azure Repos**, and the app is built and tested automatically using **Visual Studio App Center** and deployed to both **Google Play Store** and **Apple App Store** via **Fastlane**.

- **Deployment Process**:
  1. Developers push code to **Azure Repos**.
  2. **Azure DevOps** builds the Xamarin app.
  3. **App Center** is used to run unit tests and deploy the app to both Android and iOS devices for testing.
  4. The app is then automatically uploaded to the **Google Play Store** and **Apple App Store** for production release.

3. Microservices (Python + Flask, C# + ASP.NET Core)

- A **microservices architecture** consisting of both **Python Flask** and **C# ASP.NET Core** services is deployed to **Kubernetes**. The CI/CD pipeline, managed through **CircleCI** and **Helm**, automates the deployment of individual services.

- **Deployment Process**:

145

1. Each service is developed and committed to a shared **GitHub** repository.
2. **CircleCI** triggers the pipeline, which builds Docker images for both Flask and ASP.NET Core services.
3. The services are tested using **pytest** (for Python) and **xUnit** (for C#).
4. The Docker images are deployed to a **Kubernetes** cluster, with traffic routed via **Istio** for microservices management.

Key Takeaways

- **CI/CD** practices automate the process of integrating, testing, and deploying code, ensuring faster and more reliable releases.
- **Python** and **C#** offer a variety of tools and frameworks to implement CI/CD pipelines, such as **GitHub Actions**, **Azure DevOps**, and **CircleCI**.
- **Real-life examples** highlight how CI/CD pipelines can be used to automate the deployment of cross-platform applications, whether they are web apps, mobile apps, or microservices.

By incorporating CI/CD into your development workflow, you can improve the speed, reliability, and consistency of your cross-platform application development, ensuring that new features and bug fixes are deployed quickly and safely to all users.

CHAPTER 14

MANAGING API INTEGRATIONS

Working with APIs Across Different Platforms

APIs (Application Programming Interfaces) are an essential part of modern software applications, enabling communication and data exchange between different systems. In cross-platform development, APIs are used to integrate various components, services, and third-party applications, ensuring that all platforms (e.g., web, mobile, desktop) can access the necessary data and functionality.

When working with APIs across different platforms, developers face the challenge of ensuring that the communication between components remains seamless, secure, and efficient. Key considerations for managing API integrations across platforms include:

1. **Consistency in Data Handling**:
   o Ensure that data is handled consistently across different platforms, both in terms of structure (e.g., JSON format) and behavior (e.g., error handling and response formats). APIs should be designed to work well across multiple platforms

without requiring platform-specific modifications.

2. **Authentication and Authorization**:

   o Secure communication between platforms is crucial. Common authentication methods like **OAuth 2.0** and **JWT (JSON Web Tokens)** can be used to manage user authentication and ensure secure access to API endpoints, regardless of whether the app is running on Android, iOS, or the web.

3. **Network Handling**:

   o Cross-platform apps often need to deal with varying network conditions, including slow or intermittent internet connections. It is essential to implement techniques like **retry logic**, **caching**, and **offline support** to ensure smooth communication between platforms when network conditions are unreliable.

4. **Error Handling**:

   o APIs should return consistent and informative error messages that can be easily parsed by cross-platform applications. It's essential to standardize the error-handling mechanism to provide a consistent experience for the user, regardless of the platform.

5. **Versioning**:

o APIs are often updated over time, and cross-platform apps must handle changes in API versions. It's essential to implement API versioning strategies to avoid breaking changes and ensure backward compatibility across platforms.

RESTful vs. GraphQL APIs in Cross-Platform Architecture

APIs can generally be categorized into **RESTful** APIs and **GraphQL** APIs, each of which has its strengths and use cases. In cross-platform development, the choice between RESTful and GraphQL APIs can significantly affect how data is retrieved and managed across platforms.

1. RESTful APIs

- **Overview**: REST (Representational State Transfer) is a traditional architectural style for building APIs. It relies on standard HTTP methods (GET, POST, PUT, DELETE) and uses stateless communication, meaning each request contains all the information needed to understand and process the request. RESTful APIs typically return data in a consistent format, such as **JSON** or **XML**.
- **Advantages**:

- o **Simplicity**: REST APIs are simple to implement and understand. They follow a standard set of rules and are widely supported across platforms.

- o **HTTP-based**: REST APIs use standard HTTP methods, making them easy to integrate with any platform that can make HTTP requests.

- o **Cacheable**: Responses from REST APIs can be cached, which improves performance, especially for read-heavy applications.

- o **Scalability**: REST APIs scale well because they are stateless, meaning each request is independent, and there is no need to store session information on the server.

- **Disadvantages**:

  - o **Over-fetching and Under-fetching**: REST APIs often return large amounts of data, even when only a small portion is needed. This can lead to over-fetching, where more data is retrieved than necessary. Conversely, under-fetching occurs when an endpoint doesn't return enough data, requiring multiple requests.

  - o **Fixed Responses**: REST APIs have predefined endpoints, which may not be flexible enough for all use cases.

- **Use Cases**:

o   RESTful APIs are well-suited for applications that require simple, predictable, and stateless communication. They work well for services like user authentication, data retrieval, and CRUD operations.

2. GraphQL APIs

- **Overview**: GraphQL is a query language for APIs that allows clients to request exactly the data they need, and nothing more. Unlike REST, GraphQL APIs expose a single endpoint, and the client can specify which fields and data it wants to retrieve in a single request.

- **Advantages**:
  - **Efficient Data Retrieval**: GraphQL solves the problem of over-fetching and under-fetching by allowing the client to request exactly the data it needs. This can be particularly beneficial in cross-platform development, where each platform may need different data structures.
  - **Single Endpoint**: GraphQL uses a single endpoint for all requests, making it easier to manage and maintain compared to RESTful APIs, which require multiple endpoints for different resources.

- **Flexible and Customizable**: GraphQL provides more flexibility because it allows clients to request complex data in one query. This is useful when working with multiple platforms that may need different data structures.
- **Real-time Data with Subscriptions**: GraphQL supports real-time data updates using subscriptions, which can be useful in applications that require real-time communication (e.g., messaging or collaborative apps).

- **Disadvantages**:
  - **Complexity**: GraphQL APIs can be more complex to implement and maintain than REST APIs, especially for developers who are unfamiliar with the query language.
  - **Overhead**: Since the client has to specify exactly what data it needs, GraphQL queries can be more resource-intensive, leading to potential performance issues in certain cases.
  - **Caching Complexity**: While REST APIs can be easily cached with HTTP methods, caching in GraphQL requires additional setup, making it harder to implement efficient caching.

- **Use Cases**:
  - GraphQL is well-suited for cross-platform apps that require flexible and efficient data retrieval.

It's ideal for applications with dynamic or complex data models, where clients need to request specific pieces of data tailored to their needs. Examples include social media apps, real-time collaboration apps, or e-commerce platforms.

Python and C# Libraries for Seamless API Integration

Both Python and C# provide powerful libraries to integrate APIs smoothly, making it easy for developers to build, manage, and consume APIs in their applications.

Python Libraries for API Integration

1. **Requests**:
    - o **Overview**: The **requests** library is one of the most popular Python libraries for making HTTP requests. It is simple to use and handles all the complexities of making HTTP calls and managing responses.
    - o **Usage**: The requests library is commonly used to integrate RESTful APIs, send GET, POST, PUT, DELETE requests, and handle responses.
    - o **Example**:

    ```python
    python
    ```

```
import requests

response                          =
requests.get('https://api.example.c
om/data')
if response.status_code == 200:
    data = response.json()
    print(data)
```

2. **Graphene**:
   o **Overview**: **Graphene** is a Python library for building GraphQL APIs. It provides a powerful framework for creating and consuming GraphQL APIs in Python applications.
   o **Usage**: Graphene allows Python developers to easily integrate GraphQL into their applications, enabling efficient data retrieval and real-time updates.
   o **Example**:

```
python

import graphene

class Query(graphene.ObjectType):
    hello = graphene.String()

    def resolve_hello(self, info):
```

```
return 'Hello, world!'
```

```
schema                              =
graphene.Schema(query=Query)
result = schema.execute('{ hello }')
print(result.data['hello'])
```

3. Flask-GraphQL:

- o **Overview**: **Flask-GraphQL** is an extension for Flask that integrates GraphQL with Flask applications. It makes it easy to expose a GraphQL endpoint and manage API calls.
- o **Usage**: Flask-GraphQL allows Flask developers to build powerful GraphQL APIs quickly and efficiently.
- o **Example**:

```python

from flask import Flask
from        flask_graphql        import
GraphQLView
from graphene import Schema

app = Flask(__name__)

class Query(graphene.ObjectType):
    hello = graphene.String()
```

156

```
def resolve_hello(self, info):
    return 'Hello, Flask!'


schema = Schema(query=Query)


app.add_url_rule('/graphql',
view_func=GraphQLView.as_view('grap
hql', schema=schema, graphiql=True))


if __name__ == '__main__':
    app.run()
```

C# Libraries for API Integration

1. **HttpClient**:

   o **Overview**: The **HttpClient** class in C# is part of the **System.Net.Http** namespace and provides a simple API for sending HTTP requests and receiving responses. It is commonly used for integrating RESTful APIs in C# applications.

   o **Usage**: **HttpClient** is ideal for making asynchronous HTTP calls, allowing C# developers to interact with APIs easily.

   o **Example**:

```csharp
csharp


using System.Net.Http;
using System.Threading.Tasks;
```

157

```csharp
public async Task GetDataFromAPI()
{
    HttpClient client = new HttpClient();
    HttpResponseMessage response = await
client.GetAsync("https://api.exampl
e.com/data");
    if
(response.IsSuccessStatusCode)
    {
        string data = await
response.Content.ReadAsStringAsync(
);
        Console.WriteLine(data);
    }
}
```

2. GraphQL.Client:

- o **Overview**: **GraphQL.Client** is a C# library for interacting with GraphQL APIs. It simplifies sending GraphQL queries and parsing responses in C# applications.
- o **Usage**: **GraphQL.Client** is useful for developers who want to consume GraphQL APIs from C#.
- o **Example**:

```
csharp
```

```
var        client      =        new
GraphQLHttpClient("https://api.exam
ple.com/graphql");
var request = new GraphQLRequest
{
    Query = "{ users { name } }"
};

var       response      =       await
client.SendQueryAsync<MyQueryRespon
se>(request);
```

3. **RestSharp**:

   o **Overview**: **RestSharp** is a popular C# library for making RESTful API requests. It simplifies interacting with REST APIs and handling responses, including authentication, error handling, and JSON parsing.

   o **Usage**: **RestSharp** is used for integrating RESTful APIs quickly and efficiently, handling various HTTP methods like GET, POST, PUT, DELETE.

   o **Example**:

```
csharp
```

159

```
var          client          =          new
RestClient("https://api.example.com
");
var          request          =          new
RestRequest("data", Method.GET);
var          response          =          await
client.ExecuteAsync(request);
if (response.IsSuccessful)
{

Console.WriteLine(response.Content)
;
}
```

Key Takeaways

- **APIs** are a crucial component in cross-platform development, providing communication and data exchange between different systems and platforms.
- The choice between **RESTful APIs** and **GraphQL** depends on the specific needs of the application. **REST** is simple and predictable, while **GraphQL** offers flexibility and efficiency in data retrieval.
- Both **Python** and **C#** offer robust libraries for integrating APIs, such as **Requests** and **Flask-GraphQL** for Python, and **HttpClient** and **RestSharp** for C#.

By selecting the right API technology and libraries, developers can efficiently integrate and manage APIs across different platforms, ensuring seamless communication and functionality in cross-platform applications.

CHAPTER 15

UI/UX DESIGN IN CROSS-PLATFORM APPLICATIONS

Designing Intuitive User Interfaces for Multiple Platforms

In cross-platform development, one of the primary challenges is designing user interfaces (UI) that work seamlessly across various platforms (e.g., desktop, mobile, web). A good user interface isn't just about aesthetics; it's about creating a smooth, efficient, and enjoyable user experience (UX). This becomes even more important when you're working across platforms with different screen sizes, input methods (e.g., touch, mouse, keyboard), and performance considerations.

1. **Platform-Specific Considerations**:
   - **Consistency**: It is essential to maintain consistency across all platforms while respecting the unique characteristics of each platform. This means your app should behave similarly across platforms but also adhere to platform-specific design guidelines. For instance, mobile applications may require larger buttons and

touch-friendly elements, while desktop versions can offer more complex layouts and interactions.

o **Adaptability**: The user interface should be adaptive, ensuring that it adjusts to different screen sizes, orientations, and input methods. A mobile device might need a simplified view with larger text and controls, while a desktop app can display more detailed content.

o **Responsive Design**: Designing with responsive design principles ensures that the UI adjusts dynamically based on screen size and resolution, providing an optimal experience on all devices, whether it's a smartphone, tablet, or desktop.

2. **User Experience (UX)**:

o UX design in cross-platform development should focus on making interactions intuitive and seamless across all platforms. This includes:

▪ **Navigation**: Navigation elements like menus and buttons should be easy to find and use. Mobile apps often use bottom navigation bars, while desktop apps might use sidebars or dropdown menus.

▪ **Loading Speed**: Ensure that the app performs efficiently across platforms. Slow loading times or laggy animations can severely affect the user experience.

- **Consistency in Feedback**: Users should receive immediate feedback for their actions, such as confirmation when an action is successful or clear error messages when something goes wrong.

- **User Testing**: Conduct usability testing on all target platforms to identify pain points and improve the overall experience. Testing should involve real users to ensure the design is intuitive.

3. **Cross-Platform User Interfaces**:

   o One of the key principles in cross-platform design is to maintain a balance between **native experience** and **shared codebase**. You may use shared code for core functionality, but for UI elements, you might need to customize certain features to meet the expectations of users on each platform.

   o **Design Systems**: Design systems like **Material Design** (for Android and web) or **Human Interface Guidelines** (for iOS) help in creating consistent UI elements that are familiar to users on those platforms. A cross-platform application can leverage these design systems to ensure that the UI follows platform conventions.

164

Cross-Platform UI/UX Tools and Frameworks

Several tools and frameworks can help developers design and build intuitive user interfaces for cross-platform applications. These frameworks allow developers to write once and deploy to multiple platforms, ensuring that the application adapts to the look and feel of each platform while maintaining core functionality.

1. Flutter

- **Overview**: Developed by Google, **Flutter** is a UI toolkit that enables developers to build natively compiled applications for mobile, web, and desktop from a single codebase. Flutter allows for highly customizable and beautiful user interfaces with a rich set of pre-designed widgets.
- **Key Features**:
  - **Hot Reload**: Flutter's hot reload feature allows developers to make changes to the UI and immediately see the results without restarting the app, making UI design and iteration much faster.
  - **Material Design**: Flutter comes with built-in Material Design components, which help developers create apps that feel native on both Android and iOS.

165

- o **Custom Widgets**: You can create custom widgets in Flutter, providing the flexibility to design unique interfaces for different platforms while still maintaining consistency.

- **Use Cases**:
  - o **Mobile Apps**: Flutter is particularly popular for building mobile applications, offering a smooth and responsive user interface across both Android and iOS.
  - o **Web and Desktop**: Flutter's capability has extended to the web and desktop, allowing developers to use the same codebase across all platforms.

2. React Native

- **Overview**: **React Native** is a JavaScript framework developed by Facebook for building cross-platform mobile apps using React. It enables developers to use a single codebase for iOS and Android apps, leveraging native components and capabilities for a high-quality user experience.

- **Key Features**:
  - o **Native Performance**: React Native allows developers to write native code when needed,

ensuring high performance and access to native device features.

- o **Component-Based**: React Native follows a component-based architecture, which makes it easy to build reusable UI components and manage the app's state.

- o **Responsive Design**: With tools like **Flexbox**, developers can create responsive layouts that adapt to different screen sizes and orientations.

- **Use Cases**:

- o **Mobile Apps**: React Native is widely used for building mobile applications that need a native look and feel across both Android and iOS.

3. Xamarin

- **Overview**: **Xamarin** is a Microsoft-owned framework for building cross-platform mobile apps using **C#**. Xamarin allows developers to write shared logic in C# while designing native UIs for Android and iOS using platform-specific APIs and controls.

- **Key Features**:

- o **Native UI Components**: Xamarin uses native UI components on both Android and iOS, providing a native look and feel across platforms.

167

- o **Xamarin.Forms**: Xamarin.Forms allows developers to create cross-platform UIs using a single shared codebase. It is ideal for apps that require a consistent interface across platforms without significant customization.
- o **Access to Native APIs**: Xamarin allows developers to access platform-specific APIs for native performance and functionality when necessary.

- **Use Cases**:
  - o **Mobile Apps**: Xamarin is perfect for building mobile apps where you need full access to native functionality while still sharing most of the code across platforms.
  - o **Enterprise Applications**: Xamarin is often used for enterprise mobile applications, as it integrates well with the Microsoft ecosystem.

4. Qt

- **Overview**: **Qt** is a powerful cross-platform framework primarily used for building desktop and mobile applications in C++. It supports a wide variety of platforms, including Windows, macOS, Linux, iOS, and Android.
- **Key Features**:

- o **Rich UI Design**: Qt provides a rich set of widgets for building beautiful, interactive UIs. It also offers features like **QtQuick** and **QML** for building dynamic UIs with ease.
- o **High Performance**: Qt is highly optimized for performance, which makes it ideal for building resource-intensive applications such as games or real-time applications.
- o **Native Look and Feel**: Qt ensures that applications maintain a native look and feel on different platforms.

- **Use Cases**:
  - o **Desktop Applications**: Qt is highly popular for building cross-platform desktop applications, especially for industries that require custom graphical user interfaces (GUIs).
  - o **Embedded Systems**: Qt is also used in embedded systems and IoT applications due to its low resource consumption and flexibility.

Examples of UI/UX in Action with Python and C#

1. Python Example: Building a GUI with PyQt

PyQt is a set of Python bindings for the **Qt** application framework. It allows developers to create cross-platform desktop applications with a native look and feel. The following is a simple example of a Python application built with **PyQt5**:

```python
python

import sys
from PyQt5.QtWidgets import QApplication,
QWidget, QLabel

class MyWindow(QWidget):
    def __init__(self):
        super().__init__()
        self.setWindowTitle('PyQt5         Cross-
Platform UI')
        self.setGeometry(100, 100, 400, 300)
        label = QLabel('Hello, world!', self)
        label.move(150, 130)

if __name__ == '__main__':
    app = QApplication(sys.argv)
    window = MyWindow()
    window.show()
    sys.exit(app.exec_())
```

This code creates a basic window with a label, demonstrating how easy it is to build a native desktop application with PyQt that can run across different platforms.

2. C# Example: Xamarin.Forms Mobile Application

In **Xamarin.Forms**, developers can create cross-platform mobile applications using a shared UI codebase. The following example demonstrates a simple Xamarin.Forms application that runs on both iOS and Android:

```csharp
using Xamarin.Forms;

namespace CrossPlatformApp
{
    public class App : Application
    {
        public App()
        {
            MainPage = new ContentPage
            {
                Content = new Label
                {
                    Text = "Hello, Xamarin!",
                    HorizontalOptions       =
LayoutOptions.Center,
                    VerticalOptions         =
LayoutOptions.Center
                }
            };
        }
```

```
    }
}
```

This app will display a "Hello, Xamarin!" label centered on the screen, demonstrating the simplicity and power of Xamarin.Forms for building cross-platform UIs.

Key Takeaways

- **UI/UX design** in cross-platform applications requires balancing platform-specific features and maintaining consistency across devices.
- **Cross-platform UI frameworks** like **Flutter**, **React Native**, **Xamarin**, and **Qt** offer tools to build intuitive and responsive user interfaces for multiple platforms, helping developers streamline the design and development process.
- **Python** and **C#** provide robust libraries and frameworks (e.g., **PyQt**, **Xamarin.Forms**) for building cross-platform applications with native look-and-feel UIs.

By using the right tools and principles, developers can design cross-platform applications that provide excellent user experiences across different platforms, leading to increased user satisfaction and engagement.

CHAPTER 16

TROUBLESHOOTING CROSS-PLATFORM ISSUES

Common Challenges Faced in Cross-Platform Development

Cross-platform development offers the advantage of reducing the amount of code you need to write and maintain for different platforms, but it also comes with its own set of challenges. Developers often encounter issues related to platform compatibility, performance, and debugging, which can make cross-platform applications difficult to maintain and optimize.

Here are some common challenges faced in cross-platform development:

1. **Platform-Specific Behavior**:
   - Every platform (e.g., Android, iOS, Windows, macOS) has its own set of behaviors, APIs, and limitations. These differences can lead to inconsistent user experiences and functionality between platforms. For example, Android might handle certain UI elements differently than iOS,

or one platform might support a feature that another does not.

- o **Solution**: Ensure that platform-specific code is used when necessary and that the app's behavior is tested on all target platforms. Use design patterns like **dependency injection** to separate platform-specific logic from the core app logic.

2. **User Interface Inconsistencies**:

- o Cross-platform apps must ensure that the user interface (UI) looks and behaves consistently across platforms. However, each platform has its own design conventions and UI elements (e.g., Android's Material Design vs. iOS's Human Interface Guidelines).

- o **Solution**: Use **platform-specific UI components** or frameworks (e.g., **Xamarin.Forms**, **Flutter**, **React Native**) to create consistent and responsive layouts. Ensure that UI components adapt to different screen sizes and orientations.

3. **Performance Issues**:

- o Cross-platform apps might face performance degradation due to the abstraction layers required to make them compatible across multiple platforms. This can lead to slower startup times, sluggish animations, or inefficient handling of resources like memory and CPU.

- o **Solution**: Optimize the app's performance by identifying bottlenecks with profiling tools. Use **native code** when necessary for performance-critical tasks, or consider using **native modules** to optimize specific functionalities.

4. **Third-Party Library Compatibility**:

- o When using third-party libraries or APIs, compatibility can become an issue. Libraries that work well on one platform might not be supported or behave as expected on another.
- o **Solution**: Carefully select third-party libraries with cross-platform support. Use libraries that are actively maintained and regularly updated, and ensure that they support your target platforms.

5. **Networking and Connectivity Issues**:

- o Cross-platform apps often rely on network communication to sync data and interact with remote services. Differences in networking APIs or handling of offline scenarios (e.g., caching, sync) between platforms can lead to connectivity issues.
- o **Solution**: Use **platform-independent networking libraries** (e.g., **Retrofit** for Android, **Alamofire** for iOS) to ensure consistent

networking behavior across platforms. Implement offline support with local databases or caching systems.

6. **Handling Device-Specific Hardware and Features**:

   o Different platforms provide varying levels of access to device hardware (e.g., camera, GPS, accelerometer). Certain features may be more easily accessible on one platform than on another.

   o **Solution**: Use platform-specific APIs when needed, or leverage cross-platform libraries (e.g., **Xamarin Essentials**, **Flutter plugins**, **React Native modules**) to access device features consistently.

Debugging Tools and Strategies

When issues arise during cross-platform development, debugging tools and strategies become invaluable in identifying and fixing bugs. Below are some essential tools and strategies for debugging cross-platform apps:

1. **Common Debugging Strategies**:

   o **Reproduce the Issue**: Before debugging, try to reproduce the issue consistently across platforms. Make sure the bug appears on both the development environment and the target platform.

o **Divide and Conquer**: Break down the problem into smaller sections by isolating parts of the code. Narrow down the cause of the issue by disabling certain features or logic to determine where the issue originates.

o **Log Everything**: Use logging extensively during development. Logs provide valuable insights into what's happening in the app and where it's failing. Make sure logs are platform-agnostic and output in a consistent format across platforms.

2. **Platform-Specific Debugging Tools**:

o **Android Studio and Xcode**: For mobile apps, **Android Studio** (for Android) and **Xcode** (for iOS) offer powerful debugging tools, such as device simulators, real-time log viewers, and memory profiling.

o **Chrome Developer Tools**: For web applications, **Chrome DevTools** offers various debugging features, including inspecting HTML/CSS, monitoring network activity, and checking for performance issues.

o **VS Code**: **Visual Studio Code** supports debugging across different languages (Python, C#, JavaScript) with extensions for each platform, providing a unified debugging environment.

3. **Cross-Platform Debugging Tools**:

   o **Flutter DevTools**: For Flutter apps, **Flutter DevTools** provides a suite of debugging tools that help analyze performance, inspect the widget tree, view logs, and more.

   o **React Native Debugger**: **React Native Debugger** is a standalone app for debugging React Native apps. It integrates with the React DevTools, allowing you to inspect components, monitor network requests, and view Redux state.

   o **Xamarin Profiler**: **Xamarin Profiler** is a tool used to measure and improve the performance of your Xamarin apps. It helps to identify memory leaks, CPU usage, and other performance bottlenecks across platforms.

   o **Postman**: For testing and debugging API calls, **Postman** allows developers to send requests, monitor responses, and simulate various network conditions.

4. **Profiling and Performance Tools**:

   o **Flame Graphs**: Tools like **Flamegraph** can visualize performance bottlenecks in an app. This is particularly useful for identifying inefficient areas in cross-platform apps that may have performance issues.

o **Google Chrome Lighthouse**: Lighthouse is an open-source tool for auditing web apps, providing insights into performance, accessibility, SEO, and more. It's helpful for ensuring that cross-platform web applications are optimized.

o **Appium**: For cross-platform mobile apps, **Appium** allows you to write tests for mobile applications and track performance while automating tests.

How to Address Platform-Specific Issues with Python and C#

Despite best efforts, platform-specific issues will arise. Below are some approaches to handling these issues when working with **Python** and **C#**.

Platform-Specific Solutions in Python:

1. **Using Conditional Imports**:

   o Python provides the ability to handle platform-specific code by using conditional imports or platform checks.

   o **Example**:

```python
import platform

if platform.system() == 'Darwin':
    import mac_specific_library
elif platform.system() == 'Windows':
    import windows_specific_library
else:
    import general_library
```

2. **Third-Party Libraries**:

   o Many cross-platform libraries provide ways to access platform-specific functionality. For example, **PyQt** allows you to create native UIs while handling platform-specific behaviors (e.g., for macOS vs. Windows).

   o **Example**:

   ▪ To access the system clipboard in Python, you might use **pyperclip** for cross-platform clipboard handling. But if specific behavior is needed for one platform, you can include platform-specific checks.

3. **Using Platform-Specific Extensions**:

   o If you need direct access to hardware (e.g., camera, GPS), you might need to write platform-specific code. Libraries like **Kivy** for mobile or

PyInstaller for packaging apps allow you to target platform-specific features.

1. **Using Dependency Injection**:
   - C# and **Xamarin** allow developers to inject platform-specific implementations into their code using **dependency injection**. This helps decouple platform-specific code from shared logic.
   - **Example**:

```csharp
public                  interface
IPlatformSpecificService
{
    void PerformPlatformAction();
}

public class PlatformSpecificService
: IPlatformSpecificService
{
    public                  void
PerformPlatformAction()
    {
        // Platform-specific logic
    }
}
```

181

```
// Register in the Dependency
Injection container
builder.Services.AddSingleton<IPlat
formSpecificService,
PlatformSpecificService>();
```

2. **Platform-Specific Code Using #if Preprocessor Directives**:

- o In C#, **preprocessor directives** like #if allow developers to write platform-specific code within the same file.
- o **Example**:

```csharp
csharp

#if ANDROID
    // Android-specific code
#elif IOS
    // iOS-specific code
#else
    // Code for other platforms
#endif
```

3. **Using Xamarin Essentials**:

- o **Xamarin Essentials** is a cross-platform library that simplifies platform-specific functionality, such as GPS, camera, and secure storage, while handling platform-specific differences under the hood.

4. **Debugging with Visual Studio**:
   - **Visual Studio** provides a comprehensive suite of debugging tools, allowing developers to test and debug their cross-platform code on simulators/emulators for different platforms. The **Xamarin Inspector** and **Live Reload** features allow for quick testing and troubleshooting.

Key Takeaways

- **Cross-platform development** presents common challenges such as platform-specific behavior, performance issues, UI inconsistencies, and network connectivity problems.
- **Debugging tools** like **Flutter DevTools**, **Xamarin Profiler**, and **Chrome DevTools** help developers pinpoint and resolve cross-platform issues.
- **Platform-specific solutions** in **Python** and **C#** can be implemented using conditional code, dependency injection, or preprocessor directives to ensure that the app performs optimally on all platforms.

By using the right debugging tools, strategies, and platform-specific solutions, developers can effectively troubleshoot and resolve issues in cross-platform applications, ensuring they work smoothly and efficiently across all target platforms.

CHAPTER 17

FUTURE TRENDS IN CROSS-PLATFORM ARCHITECTURE

The Future of Cross-Platform Development

Cross-platform development has come a long way from its early days, and the future promises even more exciting advancements. As the demand for applications that work seamlessly across various devices and platforms increases, the focus is shifting towards improving the efficiency, performance, and user experience of cross-platform apps.

Here are some key trends shaping the future of cross-platform development:

1. **Unified Development Models**:
   - **Single Codebase, Multiple Platforms**: The push for having a single codebase that works across all platforms (mobile, desktop, web, embedded) is gaining momentum. Frameworks like **Flutter**, **React Native**, **Xamarin**, and **Electron** will continue to evolve, enabling developers to write once and deploy on multiple platforms without sacrificing performance or user experience.

185

- o **Cross-Platform UIs**: New advancements in **UI frameworks** will enable even more robust, flexible, and platform-agnostic designs. The goal is to minimize the differences between native and cross-platform UIs, allowing for a consistent and performant experience.

2. **Serverless Architectures**:

- o The shift toward **serverless computing** is another trend in cross-platform development. Serverless computing abstracts the underlying infrastructure and lets developers focus on writing code without worrying about servers. Platforms like **AWS Lambda**, **Azure Functions**, and **Google Cloud Functions** are making it easier to build scalable, event-driven applications across multiple platforms.

- o **Cross-Platform Backend Services**: As serverless architectures become more mainstream, backend-as-a-service (BaaS) platforms like **Firebase** and **AWS Amplify** will play a critical role in simplifying the backend development for cross-platform apps.

3. **Low-Code and No-Code Development**:

- o **Low-code** and **no-code** platforms will significantly impact cross-platform development by allowing developers to build applications with minimal hand-coding. These platforms provide drag-and-drop components and pre-built integrations, speeding up development and enabling non-developers to participate in app creation.

- o **Cross-Platform App Builders**: Tools like **OutSystems**, **Appgyver**, and **Bubble** are helping businesses quickly build cross-platform applications without deep technical knowledge, opening doors for rapid prototyping and faster development cycles.

4. **5G and Edge Computing**:

- o The rollout of **5G** networks will drastically improve the performance of cross-platform apps by enabling faster data transfer, low latency, and better real-time communication. This is particularly important for applications that rely on real-time data, such as gaming, video conferencing, and augmented reality (AR).

- o **Edge Computing**: As **edge computing** becomes more prevalent, cross-platform applications will increasingly leverage computing resources closer to the user, reducing latency and improving performance for real-time applications.

5. **Progressive Web Apps (PWAs)**:

- o **PWAs** are gaining traction as they combine the best aspects of native apps and web apps. PWAs are responsive, fast, and can be installed directly from the browser without going through app stores, making them an excellent choice for cross-platform development.

- o With more web technologies supporting native-like experiences, PWAs will continue to evolve and gain wider acceptance as a cross-platform solution.

Emerging Technologies (e.g., AI, Machine Learning) in Cross-Platform Apps

The integration of **emerging technologies** into cross-platform applications is accelerating. Technologies such as **AI**, **machine learning (ML)**, **augmented reality (AR)**, **blockchain**, and **IoT** are transforming how cross-platform apps are built and how users interact with them.

1. **Artificial Intelligence (AI) and Machine Learning (ML):**

   - o **AI and ML** are poised to become integral components of cross-platform apps, enhancing personalization, automating tasks, and improving decision-making. For instance, AI can help customize the user experience by learning from user behavior and predicting their preferences across multiple platforms.

- o **AI-powered Chatbots and Voice Assistants**: Integrating **AI-driven chatbots** (e.g., **Google Assistant**, **Amazon Alexa**) into cross-platform applications will streamline user interactions and provide more engaging experiences. Similarly, **voice recognition** features will be enhanced, making it easier to control apps across devices through natural language.

- o **On-device AI/ML**: With the power of modern devices (smartphones, wearables, desktops), many cross-platform apps will begin leveraging **on-device AI/ML** for features like real-time image recognition, predictive text, or offline language translation.

2. **Augmented Reality (AR)**:

- o **AR** is increasingly being integrated into mobile applications for immersive experiences. Cross-platform frameworks like **Unity** and **ARCore** (Android) or **ARKit** (iOS) make it easier to develop AR experiences that work across multiple platforms. For example, AR can be used for virtual try-ons in shopping apps, real-time object scanning in industrial applications, and interactive gaming experiences.

- o As AR technology improves, cross-platform apps will incorporate more real-time and interactive elements, allowing users to engage in richer, more dynamic environments across devices.

3. **Blockchain**:

- o **Blockchain technology** is being explored for its potential to secure data, facilitate transparent transactions, and create decentralized applications (dApps) that work seamlessly across platforms. Blockchain is particularly valuable in industries like finance, healthcare, and supply chain management, where data integrity and transparency are essential.
- o Cross-platform frameworks are enabling blockchain-based apps to run smoothly across mobile, desktop, and web environments, creating secure ecosystems for data exchange and transaction processing.

4. **IoT (Internet of Things)**:

- o With the increasing number of connected devices, **IoT** is revolutionizing cross-platform applications by enabling them to interact with sensors, wearables, home automation systems, and industrial equipment. For example, a cross-platform app can control smart home devices on both iOS and Android, ensuring a unified experience across platforms.

o Cross-platform IoT apps are increasingly being built using frameworks like **Flutter**, **React Native**, and **Xamarin**, which can interface with devices via common protocols like **Bluetooth**, **Wi-Fi**, and **Zigbee**.

How Python and C# Are Evolving for the Next Generation of Software

Both **Python** and **C#** have been instrumental in cross-platform development, and as technology continues to evolve, both languages are adapting to meet the needs of the next generation of software applications.

Python:

1. **Python in AI, Data Science, and ML**:

    o Python has become the **de facto language** for AI, ML, and data science due to its simplicity, rich libraries (like **TensorFlow**, **PyTorch**, **scikit-learn**, **Pandas**, and **NumPy**), and vibrant community. As cross-platform development increasingly incorporates AI and ML, Python's role will only grow stronger.

191

- o **TensorFlow.js** and **PyTorch Mobile** enable Python-based machine learning models to run in the browser and on mobile devices, making Python an essential tool for building intelligent cross-platform applications.

2. **Python for Mobile Development**:

- o Python traditionally has not been the go-to language for mobile app development, but this is changing with frameworks like **Kivy, BeeWare**, and **PyQt**. These frameworks allow Python developers to build cross-platform mobile applications.

- o **Pyto** and **BeeWare** are helping Python evolve into a language that can target multiple platforms, including mobile, making it possible for Python developers to create native applications.

3. **Python and Cloud-Native Development**:

- o Python's flexibility and ease of use make it ideal for cloud-native development. As cloud platforms like **AWS, Google Cloud**, and **Azure** grow, Python's role in building microservices, serverless functions, and automation scripts is expanding. **AWS Lambda**, for example, supports Python, enabling developers to run serverless functions in a cloud environment.

C#:

1. **C# for Cross-Platform Mobile Development**:
   o **Xamarin** continues to be a popular choice for cross-platform mobile development with **C#**. With the upcoming release of **MAUI** (Multi-platform App UI), Microsoft is providing a more powerful framework for building cross-platform apps with a single codebase that runs on iOS, Android, macOS, and Windows.
   o **C#** has become the go-to language for building mobile apps, especially with the rich ecosystem provided by **Visual Studio**, **Xamarin**, and now **MAUI**.

2. **C# for Cloud and Microservices**:
   o C# has a strong presence in the **cloud-native** and **microservices** architecture space. With **ASP.NET Core**, **C#** is one of the leading languages for building scalable, high-performance web APIs and microservices that can run on **Azure**, **AWS**, and **Google Cloud**.
   o **.NET 5** and **.NET 6** have further improved C#'s performance, making it a strong candidate for building efficient and scalable applications that span across multiple platforms.

3. **C# and Gaming**:

193

o **Unity**, one of the most popular game engines, uses **C#** as its primary scripting language, making it an essential tool for building cross-platform games. With **Unity's support** for mobile, console, and PC platforms, C# continues to be a central technology in the gaming industry, and cross-platform game development will continue to thrive in this space.

Key Takeaways

- The future of cross-platform development includes **unified codebases**, **serverless architectures**, **low-code/no-code platforms**, and improved **5G/edge computing** that will make apps faster and more responsive.
- **Emerging technologies** like **AI**, **ML**, **AR**, **blockchain**, and **IoT** are already becoming integral parts of cross-platform apps, and both **Python** and **C#** are evolving to meet these demands.
- **Python** continues to dominate in **AI**, **data science**, and **cloud-native development**, while **C#** is gaining ground in **mobile development**, **cloud services**, and **game development**.

By leveraging the strengths of Python and C#, developers can stay ahead of the curve and build the next generation of cross-platform applications that harness the power of emerging technologies.

CHAPTER 18

BUILDING CROSS-PLATFORM MOBILE APPLICATIONS

Developing Mobile Apps Using Python and C#

Developing cross-platform mobile applications is a crucial area in modern software development. With the rise of mobile-first applications and the need to support both Android and iOS platforms without duplicating efforts, cross-platform frameworks provide an efficient solution. Both **Python** and **C#** are viable options for building mobile apps that run on multiple platforms, leveraging tools and frameworks that allow developers to write a single codebase for different environments.

Developing Mobile Apps with Python

While Python isn't traditionally known for mobile development, the rise of frameworks like **Kivy**, **BeeWare**, and **PyQt** has opened up new possibilities. Python is an excellent choice for rapid development and prototyping, and with the right frameworks, it can be used to create fully functional mobile apps.

- **Kivy**:
  - **Overview**: **Kivy** is an open-source Python library that allows developers to build cross-platform applications for Windows, Linux, macOS, iOS, and Android. It supports multi-touch events, gestures, and other mobile-specific features.
  - **Key Features**:
    - **Rich UI Elements**: Kivy provides a wide range of customizable UI elements (buttons, labels, text inputs, sliders, etc.) for creating native-like user interfaces.
    - **Multi-touch Support**: Kivy's built-in support for multi-touch makes it ideal for mobile app development.
    - **Cross-Platform**: Write once and run on multiple platforms, including mobile devices.
    - **Use Cases**: Best suited for apps that require complex UIs or multimedia capabilities, such as games, educational apps, or data visualization tools.
  - **Example** (Kivy mobile app):

```python
python
```

```
from kivy.app import App
from kivy.uix.button import Button

class MyApp(App):
    def build(self):
        return  Button(text='Hello,
World!')

if __name__ == '__main__':
    MyApp().run()
```

- o **Challenges with Kivy**:
  - Performance can be a limitation for apps that require high computing power, such as games or complex visualizations.
  - There are some platform-specific limitations, especially with integration into native device features (like camera or GPS).

- **BeeWare**:
  - o **Overview**: **BeeWare** allows Python developers to write native apps using Python code for Android, iOS, macOS, and Windows. BeeWare provides a toolkit for creating native UIs and accessing native device features.
  - o **Key Features**:

- **Native Look and Feel**: BeeWare allows the app to use native controls and UI elements for a more integrated experience across platforms.
- **Extensible**: BeeWare provides a flexible framework for integrating additional components.
- **Use Cases**: Best suited for developers looking for full access to native APIs across platforms with a minimal amount of code.

o **Challenges with BeeWare**:

- The toolkit is still in active development, and some features or plugins may not be as mature as other cross-platform tools like **Flutter** or **Xamarin**.

Developing Mobile Apps with C#

C# is one of the most powerful languages for mobile development, especially when it comes to cross-platform solutions. With the **Xamarin** framework, C# allows developers to write apps that can run on both **iOS** and **Android** using a single codebase. Xamarin provides extensive support for native mobile functionalities, making it a great choice for building high-performance mobile apps.

199

- **Xamarin**:
  - **Overview**: **Xamarin** is a Microsoft-owned framework that allows developers to build cross-platform mobile apps using **C#**. Xamarin provides tools for creating native UIs and accessing device-specific APIs while sharing code across multiple platforms.
  - **Key Features**:
    - **Native Performance**: Xamarin allows developers to access platform-specific APIs, enabling high-performance apps with a native feel.
    - **Code Sharing**: You can write shared code for both iOS and Android, while still customizing the user interface for each platform using Xamarin.Forms or Xamarin.iOS/Xamarin.Android for more control.
    - **Integration with .NET**: Xamarin integrates seamlessly with the .NET ecosystem, which allows developers to leverage the rich libraries and tools available in the Microsoft ecosystem.
    - **Use Cases**: Xamarin is excellent for building feature-rich, high-performance mobile apps such as enterprise solutions,

gaming apps, and apps requiring integration with cloud services like **Azure**.

o **Example** (Xamarin.Forms mobile app):

```csharp
using Xamarin.Forms;

public class MyApp : Application
{
    public MyApp()
    {
        MainPage = new ContentPage
        {
            Content = new Label
            {
                Text = "Hello, Xamarin!",
                HorizontalOptions = LayoutOptions.Center,
                VerticalOptions = LayoutOptions.Center
            }
        };
    }
}
```

o **Challenges with Xamarin**:

- Xamarin's performance may lag behind fully native apps, especially for highly complex UIs or animations.
- You may face challenges with keeping up with the latest platform-specific features, especially when new iOS or Android updates are released.

Cross-Platform Mobile Development Frameworks

Several frameworks are available to facilitate the development of cross-platform mobile applications. Below are some of the most widely used frameworks for mobile development:

1. **Flutter**:
   - **Overview**: **Flutter**, developed by Google, is a UI toolkit for building natively compiled applications for mobile, web, and desktop from a single codebase. It uses the **Dart** language and offers a rich set of widgets that can be customized to look like native components.
   - **Advantages**:
     - **Hot Reload**: Changes in the code are instantly reflected in the app, improving development speed.

202

- **High Performance**: Flutter provides high performance by compiling to native code.
- **Customizable Widgets**: Flutter's widget-based UI system allows for a highly customizable user interface.

2. **React Native**:

   o **Overview**: **React Native** is a JavaScript framework that allows developers to build mobile apps using the **React** library. React Native apps use native components, allowing developers to write a single codebase for both iOS and Android.

   o **Advantages**:

      - **Native-Like Performance**: React Native uses native components for better performance.
      - **Large Ecosystem**: React Native benefits from the large React ecosystem, which offers a wealth of libraries and tools.
      - **Cross-Platform Compatibility**: Write once and deploy to both Android and iOS.

Real-World Mobile App Examples and Challenges

Here are a few real-world mobile app examples built using cross-platform frameworks, along with some of the challenges developers faced:

1. **Airbnb** (React Native):
   o **Challenge**: Airbnb originally used React Native to simplify development across iOS and Android. However, developers found that performance issues arose with certain features, particularly for navigation and UI complexity.
   o **Solution**: The team continued to use React Native for several features but switched to **native components** for performance-critical parts of the app.
2. **Alibaba** (Xamarin):
   o **Challenge**: Alibaba's cross-platform mobile app was originally built with Xamarin to streamline development across Android and iOS. As the app grew, the team faced challenges with keeping the app updated with the latest iOS and Android features.
   o **Solution**: The Alibaba team decided to use Xamarin for shared business logic and implemented platform-specific components for

204

UI and native integrations, which helped manage the complexity while maintaining performance.

3. **Google Ads** (Flutter):

   o **Challenge**: The Google Ads app was built using Flutter, enabling the development of a unified codebase for both Android and iOS. One of the challenges was ensuring smooth animations and UI responsiveness across platforms.

   o **Solution**: Flutter's **Skia graphics engine** enabled high-performance rendering, and the development team used Flutter's rich widget set to ensure the app was consistent across platforms while delivering a fast, responsive experience.

Key Takeaways

- **Cross-platform mobile development** offers a way to write a single codebase that runs on multiple platforms, saving development time and cost.

- Frameworks like **Xamarin**, **Kivy**, **Flutter**, and **React Native** provide powerful tools for building mobile apps that run on both **Android** and **iOS**, each with its own set of benefits and challenges.

- **Python** and **C#** offer solid libraries for mobile development, with **Kivy** and **BeeWare** being ideal for Python developers, while **Xamarin** is a mature solution for C# developers.

- **Real-world challenges** include ensuring performance, managing platform-specific features, and dealing with third-party library compatibility, but these can be overcome with the right tools and architecture.

Cross-platform mobile development continues to evolve, and by understanding the strengths and weaknesses of the available frameworks, developers can make informed decisions and build high-quality mobile applications that provide a seamless experience across multiple platforms.

CHAPTER 19

CASE STUDIES OF SUCCESSFUL CROSS-PLATFORM PROJECTS

Analysis of Successful Real-World Projects

Cross-platform development is an increasingly popular approach for businesses and developers who want to reach a wider audience without having to build separate applications for each platform. Several real-world projects have embraced cross-platform tools and frameworks to create successful applications. By examining these case studies, we can better understand the methodologies, tools, and best practices that made them successful.

This chapter analyzes a few successful cross-platform projects, breaking down the technologies, tools, and methods used to build them, and explores key lessons learned during their development.

**Case Study 1: Airbnb – React Native for Cross-Platform Mobile Development

Overview:

Airbnb, one of the largest online marketplaces for lodging and travel, originally relied on native development for both iOS and Android. However, in order to scale more effectively and maintain their app across multiple platforms, Airbnb shifted to using **React Native** for some parts of the mobile app.

Technologies and Tools Used:

- **React Native**: React Native was chosen to allow Airbnb to reuse code across both iOS and Android, reducing development time and effort.
- **Redux**: For managing the app's state across different components, Redux was used to handle application data in a consistent manner.
- **Native Modules**: In areas where React Native didn't meet performance needs (such as complex animations), Airbnb developers integrated **native modules** into their app to preserve performance.
- **Jest**: Testing of components was done using **Jest** to ensure stability across the platform.

Methodology:

- **Shared Codebase**: The decision to go with React Native allowed Airbnb to maintain a single codebase for both iOS and Android platforms, leading to faster development and simplified maintenance.

- **Gradual Transition**: The move to React Native was gradual. Airbnb didn't convert the entire app at once; instead, they started by replacing smaller, less complex sections of the app.

- **Mixed Architecture**: A combination of native code and React Native was used, depending on the specific needs of the feature. For instance, UI-heavy components that required high performance were built natively, while business logic and simpler views were handled by React Native.

Lessons Learned:

1. **Performance Optimization**: While React Native helped Airbnb deliver a cross-platform app, certain high-performance features (e.g., animations, maps) still required native code for smooth user experiences.

2. **Incremental Adoption**: A gradual shift to React Native allowed Airbnb to reduce the risk of disrupting the existing user experience and business functions.

3. **Native Code Integration**: The ability to write custom native code when needed proved to be a valuable tool for meeting performance requirements.

**Case Study 2: Instagram – Python and React for Web and Mobile Platforms

Overview:

Instagram, a leading social media platform for photo and video sharing, has a massive user base across web and mobile. While Instagram's original mobile app was built using **Objective-C** and **Java** for iOS and Android respectively, the company later transitioned to a more unified approach by incorporating **Python** for the backend and **React** for the web app, offering a seamless experience across platforms.

Technologies and Tools Used:

- **Python (Django)**: Instagram uses **Django**, a Python-based web framework, for the backend services that manage user data, uploads, and interactions on both the mobile and web platforms.
- **React**: React was introduced for the front-end of Instagram's web application to create a dynamic, fast-loading user experience.
- **React Native**: Instagram also experimented with **React Native** for certain features of the mobile app to ensure consistency with the web experience.

- **PostgreSQL**: A robust, open-source relational database that stores user data and interactions.
- **Celery**: Used for task queues in Python to handle background tasks such as sending notifications or image processing.

Methodology:

- **API-First Approach**: Instagram's transition to using React on the web was made easier by the company's **API-first** approach. By decoupling the frontend from the backend and using a RESTful API, Instagram was able to provide a consistent backend service that could be consumed by both mobile and web apps.
- **Cross-Platform Consistency**: React Native was leveraged for certain sections of the mobile app, ensuring that features shared the same look and feel as the web version.
- **Data Handling**: Python and Django's **ORM** (Object Relational Mapping) was used extensively to manage Instagram's large-scale data and user interactions.

Lessons Learned:

1. **API-First Approach**: Separating the backend from the frontend made Instagram's platform more flexible and

scalable, as different frontends (web, mobile) could easily be added or modified without affecting the backend.

2. **Leveraging React Native for Mobile**: By using **React Native** alongside traditional native development, Instagram was able to maintain platform consistency while achieving faster development times for certain features.

3. **Scalability**: Instagram's use of Python, Django, and PostgreSQL has proven to be highly scalable as the platform continues to handle millions of users and massive data growth.

**Case Study 3: Microsoft Teams – C# and Azure for Cross-Platform Collaboration

Overview:

Microsoft Teams, a team collaboration platform, is used by millions of organizations worldwide. It is available on mobile (iOS and Android), desktop (Windows and macOS), and web. Microsoft Teams uses **C#**, **Xamarin**, and **Azure** for its cross-platform development.

Technologies and Tools Used:

- **C# and .NET**: The core of Microsoft Teams is built on C# using the **.NET Core** framework, enabling developers to write code that works seamlessly across platforms.

- **Xamarin**: Xamarin is used to build mobile apps for both **iOS** and **Android**, ensuring that the same business logic and functionality are delivered across platforms.

- **Azure**: Microsoft's cloud platform is leveraged for scalability, data storage, and real-time communication features like chat and video calls.

- **SignalR**: **SignalR** is used for real-time communication in Teams, enabling live chat, instant notifications, and live collaboration between users across platforms.

- **Electron**: The desktop version of Teams is built using **Electron**, a framework for building cross-platform desktop applications using web technologies (HTML, CSS, JavaScript).

Methodology:

- **Shared Codebase**: Microsoft Teams uses **Xamarin** and **C#** to ensure that most of the business logic and functionality is shared across mobile platforms. The **Xamarin.Forms** library is used for creating a unified UI on mobile platforms while maintaining native look and feel.

- **Cloud-First Architecture**: Microsoft Teams is built around a **cloud-first** architecture, leveraging **Azure** for cloud storage and scalability, as well as to facilitate communication between users in real time.

- **Microservices**: Teams uses a **microservices architecture**, allowing individual components (like chat, video calls, file sharing, etc.) to be developed, tested, and deployed independently.

Lessons Learned:

1. **Consistency Across Platforms**: By using Xamarin for mobile and Electron for desktop, Microsoft Teams is able to maintain consistent UI and UX across all platforms, ensuring users have a unified experience regardless of the device they are using.

2. **Cloud Scalability**: Leveraging **Azure** and **microservices** for backend services allowed Microsoft Teams to scale quickly to meet the needs of businesses of all sizes, while handling millions of concurrent users in real time.

3. **Real-Time Communication**: Using **SignalR** for real-time data handling proved critical in providing instant updates and communication features, such as messaging and video conferencing.

Key Takeaways from Case Studies

1. **Platform-Specific Customization**: While using a shared codebase for multiple platforms is an advantage, there are still times when developers need to implement platform-specific customizations to meet the performance and UI expectations of each platform. A hybrid approach—combining shared logic with platform-specific customizations—is often the best solution.

2. **Gradual Transition to Cross-Platform**: Many companies, like Airbnb and Instagram, chose to gradually transition to cross-platform solutions rather than rewriting their entire codebase at once. This approach reduces the risk of breaking functionality and allows developers to continue using existing resources while gradually incorporating new technologies.

3. **API-First and Cloud-First Architectures**: Adopting an **API-first** approach (like Instagram) or **cloud-first** approach (like Microsoft Teams) allows for flexibility and scalability across platforms. This ensures that new platforms or devices can easily be supported in the future without needing significant changes to the backend.

4. **Use of Real-Time Features**: Cross-platform apps that focus on real-time interactions, like Microsoft Teams and Airbnb, leverage technologies like **SignalR** or **Firebase** to provide instant updates and smooth communication. Real-time functionality is crucial for collaborative apps, messaging apps, and social media platforms.

5. **Scalability and Performance**: As apps grow, scalability becomes a critical concern. By leveraging cloud solutions like **Azure** or **AWS**, companies ensure their apps can scale seamlessly while maintaining high performance.

By learning from these real-world case studies, developers can gain valuable insights into how to approach cross-platform app development, integrate the right technologies, and make informed decisions about the tools and frameworks that best fit their needs.

CHAPTER 20

CONCLUSION AND NEXT STEPS

Summarizing the Key Takeaways from the Book

As we conclude this journey into the world of cross-platform development, it's important to reflect on the key concepts, tools, and best practices we've covered throughout the book. Cross-platform development is a powerful strategy that allows developers to reach users on multiple platforms— mobile, web, desktop—without duplicating code for each one. However, it requires careful planning, the right set of tools, and a clear understanding of the challenges and benefits.

Here's a summary of the key takeaways from the book:

1. **Understanding Cross-Platform Development**:
    o   Cross-platform development allows you to write a single codebase for multiple platforms (iOS, Android, web, desktop), saving time and resources.
    o   The goal is to ensure consistency in functionality and user experience across platforms while

217

balancing the need for native performance and customization.

2. **Key Frameworks and Tools**:

   o We explored some of the most widely used frameworks and tools, including **Flutter, React Native, Xamarin, Kivy**, and **Electron**. Each of these tools has its strengths and is suited for different use cases, whether it's mobile apps, desktop apps, or web applications.

   o Technologies like **Django** (Python), **ASP.NET Core** (C#), and cloud services like **AWS, Azure**, and **Google Cloud** are integral in providing the backend infrastructure for scalable and secure cross-platform apps.

3. **Challenges and Solutions**:

   o Cross-platform development isn't without its challenges. We discussed issues like **platform-specific behavior, UI/UX inconsistencies, performance bottlenecks**, and **third-party library compatibility**.

   o We also covered how to approach debugging, troubleshooting, and platform-specific customizations to ensure smooth functionality and a seamless user experience across platforms.

4. **Emerging Trends and Technologies**:

o The book highlighted how emerging technologies like **AI**, **machine learning**, **blockchain**, **IoT**, and **AR** are being integrated into cross-platform apps to enhance user experiences and open up new possibilities for developers.

o We explored how **5G**, **edge computing**, and **progressive web apps (PWAs)** are shaping the future of cross-platform development, providing faster, more responsive applications.

5. **Real-World Case Studies**:

o Case studies of successful cross-platform projects such as **Airbnb**, **Instagram**, and **Microsoft Teams** illustrated how industry leaders use cross-platform frameworks to scale their applications, achieve consistent performance, and reduce development time.

Next Steps for Readers Interested in Mastering Cross-Platform Development

As a reader, you're now equipped with the foundational knowledge of cross-platform development, its tools, and its challenges. But mastering cross-platform development requires hands-on experience and continuous learning. Here are the next steps you should take to further your expertise in this area:

1. **Start Building Your Own Projects**:
   - o The best way to learn is by doing. Begin by building small-scale cross-platform apps to familiarize yourself with the tools and frameworks. Start with simple applications like to-do lists, weather apps, or news readers, and gradually increase the complexity as you become more comfortable.

2. **Choose a Framework and Specialize**:
   - o Pick a cross-platform framework to specialize in. Whether it's **Flutter, React Native, Xamarin**, or **Kivy**, mastering one tool will help you gain deeper knowledge and faster development speeds.
   - o Once you've chosen a framework, explore its documentation, community forums, and real-world examples to learn how it's used in production applications.

3. **Contribute to Open Source**:
   - o Contributing to open-source projects is a great way to gain real-world experience and improve your skills. There are numerous open-source projects related to cross-platform development that welcome contributions, and participating in these can give you insight into best practices and collaboration within a development community.

4. **Master Backend Integration**:

   o A crucial aspect of cross-platform apps is their integration with backend services. Learn how to use cloud platforms like **AWS**, **Google Cloud**, or **Azure** to build scalable backends. Dive into **RESTful APIs**, **GraphQL**, and **serverless architectures** to understand how to design backend systems that support mobile and web applications.

5. **Focus on UI/UX Design**:

   o Cross-platform UI/UX design is an area that requires special attention. Understanding how to design for multiple screen sizes, input methods, and platform guidelines will make your apps more user-friendly and professional. Study the design principles of Material Design, Apple's Human Interface Guidelines, and other design systems.

6. **Stay Updated with Emerging Trends**:

   o The world of cross-platform development is always evolving. Keep an eye on emerging technologies like **AI**, **blockchain**, and **5G**. These technologies will continue to shape the way apps are built and provide new opportunities for cross-platform developers.

7. **Seek Certifications or Formal Education**:

o For more structured learning, consider pursuing certifications in cross-platform frameworks or cloud technologies. Platforms like **Udemy**, **Coursera**, and **Pluralsight** offer courses that cover the core concepts and advanced techniques in cross-platform development.

o Attending industry conferences or meetups, whether in-person or virtual, can help you network with other professionals, stay on top of industry trends, and gain exposure to new ideas.

Resources for Further Learning

1. **Official Documentation**:
   o **Flutter**: https://flutter.dev/docs
   o **React Native**: https://reactnative.dev/docs
   o **Xamarin**: https://docs.microsoft.com/en-us/xamarin/
   o **Kivy**: https://kivy.org/doc/stable/
   o **AWS**: https://aws.amazon.com/training/
   o **Azure**: https://learn.microsoft.com/en-us/training/
   o **Google Cloud**: https://cloud.google.com/training

2. **Books**:
   o **"Flutter for Beginners"** by Alessandro Biessek – A great resource for learning Flutter from scratch.

- o **"Learning React Native"** by Bonnie Eisenman – Ideal for React Native developers looking to get into cross-platform mobile development.
- o **"Xamarin Mobile Application Development"** by Dan Hermes – Focuses on using Xamarin for cross-platform mobile apps.
- o **"Python for Data Analysis"** by Wes McKinney – A deep dive into Python, including data analysis and machine learning libraries that can be applied in cross-platform apps.

3. **Online Communities**:

- o **Stack Overflow**: Great for finding answers to specific programming questions and issues.
- o **GitHub**: Explore open-source projects and contribute to them to enhance your skills.
- o **Reddit**: Subreddits like **r/crossplatform** and **r/learnprogramming** are fantastic for discussions and resources on cross-platform development.

4. **Video Tutorials**:

- o **YouTube**: Channels like **Academind**, **Traversy Media**, and **CodeWithHarry** offer free tutorials on mobile development using Flutter, React Native, and Xamarin.

- o **Udemy**: There are numerous affordable courses that teach cross-platform development using various frameworks.

5. **Podcasts**:
   - o **Cross-Platform Development Podcasts**: Stay updated on trends and best practices by tuning into relevant podcasts like **React Native Radio**, **The Flutter Podcast**, or **Xamarin Podcast**.

6. **Meetups and Conferences**:
   - o **Google I/O** (Flutter and Android-related content)
   - o **React Conf** (for React Native and web-related content)
   - o **Microsoft Build** (for Xamarin, C#, and cloud-related topics)
   - o **Local Meetups**: Search platforms like **Meetup.com** for local or virtual cross-platform developer meetups.

Final Thoughts

Mastering cross-platform development takes time, practice, and dedication. By embracing the right frameworks, tools, and resources, you can rapidly develop applications that run on a wide range of devices, offering your users a consistent and high-quality experience across platforms. The demand for cross-platform developers is only growing, and by continuing to build on the foundation laid in this book, you'll be well on your way to mastering cross-platform development and staying ahead of industry trends.

Now, it's time for you to dive into real-world projects, apply your learning, and become an expert in cross-platform development!

www.ingramcontent.com/pod-product-compliance
Lightning Source LLC
LaVergne TN
LVHW022341060326
832902LV00022B/4164